7/17/15
Thao, when?
Go to p. 16
Dad

JENNIFER K. JORDAN

FATHERS' WISDOM

A powerful collection of stories from fathers around the world

SQUARE TREE PUBLISHING
Los Alamitos, California
squaretreepublishing.com

FATHERS' WISDOM
Copyright © 2015 by Jennifer Jordan

All Rights Reserved.

This book is protected by the copyright laws of the United States of America. No part of this publication may be reproduced, stored in a retrieval system, or transmitted, in any form or by any means- electronic, mechanical, photocopying, recording, or otherwise–without prior written permission from the author.

Scripture quotations marked (NIV) are taken from Holy Bible, New International Version®, NIV®. Copyright© 1973, 1978, 1984 by Biblica, Inc.,™ Used by permission of Zondervan. All rights reserved worldwide. www.zondervan.com

Cover Design: Brad Webster - Webster Branding & Design
Interior Design: Jonathan McGraw - jonathanmcgraw.net

ISBN: 978-0-9903190-5-4

For more information, to contact the author, or for bulk orders:
info@squaretreepublishing.com • squaretreepublishing.com

Printed in the United States of America

I dedicate this book to my father who inspired me to write it and to all the fathers of Fathers' Wisdom who have forever blessed my life with their stories of love, kindness and heart.

TABLE OF CONTENTS

INTRODUCTION ix

    My Father - The Inspiration • *Russell Jordan* 1

1. SELF-SACRIFICING

    He Kept His Word and Changed Lives • *Rev. Scott Willsey* 7
    All in the Golfing Family • *John Solheim* 11
    The Importance of Family • *Joseph Stambouli* 15
    Wisdom from a Step Dad • *Darwin Bicknell* 19

2. OPTIMISTIC

    Fatherhood and Life - Improv Style • *Greg Atkins* 27
    Hands-Off / Love-On Father • *Jerry Moore, J.D.* 33
    My Greatest Joy • *Steven Russell* 37
    My Greatest Gift • *Jessica Russell, Ph.D.* 41
    The Father-Son Relationship • *Erik Arnesen* 43

3. BALANCE

    The Coach • *Richard Miller* 49
    The Family Wheel • *Dick Parks* 53
    Loved for the "Whole Him" • *Terje Doresius* 57
    Goodbye Workaholism, Hello Family • *Rodric Rhodes, Ph.D.* .. 59
    Football to Fatherhood • *Thomas Lewis* 63

4. FAITH

    An Artist's View of Fatherhood • *Robert Senske* 71
    Fatherhood is Sacred • *J.R. Estrella* 77
    "God is My Guide" • *Stanley Mutunga, Ph.D.* 81
    Faith in Action • *William Marmion, Ph.D.* 85
    Papa Don • *Don Sprenger* 91

5. NATURAL

Paleo Dad • *Cain Credicott* 99
Safe and Serene Living in the German Countryside
   Georg Schneider, Ph.D. 105
Yoga Dad • *Gabriel Hall* 107
Natural Living • *Paul Grenier, D.C.* 111

6. HUMBLE

Go for Broke • Jim Makino 117
Reflections on Fatherhood - A Lifetime Commitment
   Brian Hurnard 121
Helpful and Kind • *Jon Meyer* 123
Integrity • *Bob Gilder* 127
A Life of Giving Back • *Hunt Harris* 133

7. INVESTING

A Father's Impact • *Chris Steinhauser* 139
The Wonder of the Universe • *Mat Kaplan* 145
Investing Wisely in Family • *Jeff Napper* 149
Education, United Families and Simplicity • *Pedro Acosta* ... 153

8. RESPECT

Celebrating Daughters • *Eliud Martinez, Ph.D.* 159
Long-Distance Fatherhood • *Nacho Ariza* 163
Habitat for Humanity • *David Howard* 165
"Marry a Good Mother" • *Ed Sewell, Ed.D.* 169

9. SERVICE

A Man of Service • *Abdullah Akbar* 175
The Gift of Being There • *Congressman Alan Lowenthal*.........181
Embracing New Ways of Seeing, Thinking and Living
  Julio Olalla..183
Travel, Talk and Choice • *Eric Jul, Ph.D.* 187

10. PATIENCE

Father of Ten • *William Jeffers, Jr.* 191
One of Ten • *Gregory Jeffers*..195
"To Love and Be Loved" • *Joe Riddick*...................................197
Love and Acceptance • *George Alp* 201

11. COMMITTED

God in All • *Bayless Conley*..207
Teen Dad to Transformed Life • *Joe Chavez*..........................215
"Post the Score" • *Jerry Cozby*..223
A Father to Count On • *Joe Jimenez* 227
The Importance of Fidelity • *Drue Boles*...............................231

12. TOLERANCE

Courage and Inspiration • *Steve Monroney*............................237
WWII Japanese-American War Relocation Center Survivor
  James Tanaka..241
Hard Work and Persistence Bring Peace • *Tomas Kovar*........245
Voice of Truth, Voice of Peace • *Bernard Savone*....................251

EPILOGUE 259

INTRODUCTION

I never knew how wise my father was until after my mother passed away from cancer in 1998. During the years that followed, I got to know my father better and was so inspired by his wisdom that I decided to write this book honoring and celebrating the special wisdom of fathers. I took on the life-altering task of interviewing fathers who were happy to share their wisdom about fatherhood and life in person, by phone, e-mails and essays. Some even sent photos of their families along with notes of encouragement for the book. A few became an extended family of sorts, calling or e-mailing me to wish me well at the holidays.

The book is divided into sections, encouraging you to read reflectively. In each section are the wonderfully rich interviews and essays of fathers from all walks of life, united by their shared humanity as fathers. Their wisdom is seen in what they have said and how they have lived. These men share valuable insights on fatherhood meant to enlighten and encourage other fathers, those who have had little or no fathering, and all who seek to live wiser lives. It is my joy as well to share their stories of tender love for their children. I thank all the magnificent fathers who generously shared their time and wisdom with me. Here's to their great wisdom and you readers who seek to learn and live it. I now invite you to enjoy your journey through *Fathers' Wisdom*.

MY FATHER–THE INSPIRATION

Jennifer Jordan
C. Russell Jordan
California

My father often described himself as "a man of few words." The few words he spoke, though, were often gems of guidance for my life, and his actions told the true tale of his wisdom. He grew up in Belmont Shore, California, the younger of two sons to a father who served in the military. He was a fun-loving, highly intellectual man whose brilliance allowed him to skip two grades in elementary school. He was an athlete and excelled in track, tennis, golf, surfing and football. Much loved by his family and friends, a bench was purchased in his honor after he passed away at one of the golf courses where he played. The inscription reads: "In Honor of Russ Jordan, Leader of the Jordanaires, 1936-2010."

My father taught me that family always comes first. He made attending my school functions and extracurricular activities a priority despite the demand of his forty-year career in education, where he served as a teacher, coach, athletic director, administrator and counselor. Amidst his busy professional life, he always made time to support my studies and did everything from listening to me practice oral book reports and poems to cheering for me at talent shows and graduations.

My father adored sports. He often played tennis and volleyball with me and attended my gymnastics meets. Once he planned a family trip and took us to the 1976 Montréal Olympics where I saw my gymnastics heroines, Olga Korbut and Nadia Comaneci. His few words were demonstrated in his actions that clearly spoke louder to me than any words ever could.

I gained a life-long love of travel and appreciation of other lands, peoples and cultures from my father. In college, he studied the German language and went on to continue his study in Germany. I followed suit in my college days by studying French and later studied in France. He had such a passion to learn and when he talked or shared his stories, time stood still.

One Christmas Eve, my father asked a friend of ours who taught history to tell the story of the 1914 Christmas Truce where French, British and German soldiers fighting on opposing sides in World War I put down their weapons and sang Silent Night and other carols in their native language. The hatred of war was momentarily stopped by a peaceful time of brotherly love. My father sang Silent Night in German (Stille Nacht) as our friend told the story. It demonstrated his knowledge of history and language, and his hope for world peace and unity. Inspired by my father, I wrote a children's book about it to encourage our youth to help build world peace.

My father taught me to be of service by his example. As a young boy, he served as a Junior Air Raid Warden in elementary school to support the war effort during World War II. He often volunteered for other worthy causes and was a regular volunteer at the local teachers' credit union. In retirement, he provided "Meals on Wheels" for house-bound people. He was happy to help anyone: family, friend or stranger.

My father was a hard worker, but he had learned not to let the cares of life weigh him down. I remember once telling him about financial concerns I had over the need for car repairs. His reply was that money wasn't so important, and the things that I thought were a crisis would one day be forgotten; I should just enjoy my life. How could I enjoy my life while facing an impending large bill, I wondered? He knew that all problems eventually pass, and that days, months, or years from now, they wouldn't really matter. It was the wisdom of age he had acquired that gave him that surety. He was right. I certainly can't remember what the car angst was at the time.

My father also taught me to have healthy relationships graced with integrity. He enjoyed a successful thirty-nine year marriage to my mother, Karin. She passed away the very month they would have celebrated their fortieth wedding anniversary. He told me that when he met her at age twenty-one, he was hit by a comet and that this comet of love grew brighter every year. He was a spontaneous free spirit, and she was a grounded planner. Their marriage was a blend of sharing and compromise where they spent time alone, with friends and other couples. He honored the marriage vow, "until death do us part."

After my mother passed away, my dad married Kathy, another delightful woman, and once again had a loving, fun-filled marriage of deep devotion and commitment. Sadly, it ended shortly due to his passing, but the love he shared with these two women inspires many seeking such relationships of selfless, honorable love.

My father had an eternal youthfulness about him and zest for life. He taught me that amidst difficulties, still live fully and in joy. When facing the cancer that eventually took his life, he fought with all his might and lived as fully as he could until he could live no more. He went to chemotherapy and then to golf. When he could no longer walk the golf course, he rode in the golf cart, and when he was too weak to swing the clubs, he rode in the golf cart watching his beloved game and enjoying the company of his good friends. When he could no longer drive, his friends made a schedule and took him to his dialysis appointments. The abundance of love that he consistently gave was happily returned.

My father's light now shines in heaven, yet his love, joy and wisdom remain my inspiration. I hope you enjoy this journey with me as we peek into the lives of other much beloved fathers and glean wisdom from the legacy they have passed on to their children.

Today, let's live in joy, for as Thoreau once said, "Surely joy is the condition of life."

1

SELF-SACRIFICING

"One of the wisest things a person can do is to open their home and heart to a child in need. After all, as my favorite bumper sticker says, 'Superman had foster parents.'"

✥

Reverend Scott Willsey

HE KEPT HIS WORD AND CHANGED LIVES

Reverend Scott Willsey
Iowa

When I first started attending summer camp, I was the worship leader and assistant camp director. Youth Camp became the highlight of my year. I enjoyed talking with the kids, working with a talented staff, and helping teenagers think about their lives and where they were headed. Youth Camp is where I met Isaac. He was sixteen years old and already six-foot four and weighed 180 pounds; and that was mostly all muscle. Everyone knew Isaac's name after the first day because he was friendly, outgoing and always in trouble with the staff. But Isaac was a good kid with a big heart.

The last day of camp was always emotional. All the people you came to know and love over the previous week were now headed home. Each year I gave my business card to a few kids and told them that if they ever needed to talk or if they needed anything, they could call me. Isaac was one of those kids. Two weeks later, Isaac called. After some small talk, he asked, "Remember when you said at camp, if there was anything you could do for me, I could call you?"

"Yes," I replied.

He then asked, "Well, I was wondering if I could come live with you?" I sat there for what seemed like an eternity. I had made this offer to kids many times and had rarely gotten a response. Now I was being put to the test. Did I really mean what I said? I asked Isaac why he wanted to live with my family. I thought he had a home. He said he did, but he was unhappy there. You see, Isaac was a foster kid and was the victim of abuse and neglect. I found out that he had been in the "system" for years. He then told stories of the most horrific abuse. One time when he and his mother lived in a car, his stepdad pointed a gun to his head, pulled the trigger and told him that the time would come when the gun would be loaded.

When Isaac came to live with me, his foster care placement was being terminated and the Department of Human Services (DHS) was looking for a new placement for him. He'd already been in five foster homes. Suddenly, my life was overrun with people: a DHS caseworker, a Behavior Disorder teacher, a psychologist, an in-home therapist/skill builder, a children's advocate, a school social worker, attorneys, paralegals, and some people that I didn't even know *what* they did, but they felt they had a say in Isaac's life. Twenty people attended the first meeting!

The caseworker said we'd all make decisions about what Isaac needed. Since his mother abandoned him, he had what psychologists call an "attachment disorder." In the most elementary terms, it means that the people who were supposed to be there for Isaac and show him love, were not. Isaac had developed certain coping skills to deal with those issues. When people grew close and he thought he was becoming attached to them, he self-destructed by offensive or annoying behaviors to break that bond. The counselor told me that when Isaac started acting out, I was to show my displeasure for the behavior while letting him know he was still loved.

I had to practice these new skills. During a fun family weekend where we were playing games and hanging out together, Isaac started irritating those around him. I told him to leave other people alone, quit instigating things, and that just because we had a bonding time together, he didn't need to sabotage it. He was part of the family, and we would love him no matter what. He looked at me quizzically and darted to his room. After a few minutes, I went to see him. Isaac was sitting on a couch, staring at the wall with his jaw slung low. I asked him what the matter was. He said, "No one has ever told me that. They all just got tired of me and sent me someplace else." I said that even when he did things that made me angry, I would always love and accept him.

This didn't solve all the problems that come with raising a foster child, but it made Isaac feel included. It was clear that he missed his mother. I remember one time when Isaac and I were discussing how he was going to spend his clothing allowance he was getting from the state. My oldest son said, "Wow, Isaac, you get a bunch of money to go out and blow on clothes. That's cool."

Isaac looked at my son with great indignation and said, "I get that money because my mom didn't want me. I'm not even sure where my dad is. You have your parents, and I would give all that money back if I had what you have." Isaac wanted what we all want: love and acceptance from those who are responsible for giving us life.

Isaac graduated from high school and got a job with an asphalt company. He travels around the country paving parking lots and going to places I'll probably never see. Do I regret having a foster child? By all means, no. It was an enriching experience for our family and taught me that opening my home was the proper decision. The experience caused me to change my profession.

Although I'm still an ordained minister, I got involved in the "system" and am now a program coordinator of a Student

Offender Program. I work with kids like Isaac every day. One of the wisest things a person can do is to open their home and heart to a child in need. After all, as my favorite bumper sticker says, "Superman had foster parents."

Today, let's keep our word and be a "super hero" to someone and change a life.

ALL IN THE GOLFING FAMILY

John Solheim
Arizona

J.J. — When I wrote the opening chapter for this book, I described the golf course bench which family and friends purchased in honor of my golf-loving father. As I continued interviewing fathers, it was serendipitous that a friend referred me to John Solheim, Chairman and CEO of PING, one of the world's most successful golf equipment manufacturing companies. Many professional golfers have won PGA tournaments with PING clubs. I interviewed John by telephone from my California condo (sitting in front of my computer looking at the PING website) while he was at his PING office in Phoenix.

—

I guess you could say that my family has made golfing more than just a past time, but a full-time business. I remember making putters in the garage with my dad, Karsten Solheim, when I was just thirteen years old. It's hard to imagine now that we once huddled over the stove, heating up putter heads, especially since that small enterprise has become PING, a world-renowned golf manufacturing company.

No matter how busy my father was then, keeping up with orders and growing his budding enterprise, he always made time for family and was a constant presence at my football games. In 1994, *Golfweek Magazine* named my dad "Golf Industry's Father of the Year." I continued working with my father until

1995, when he passed the reins onto me when he was in his early eighties. I learned not only a passion for the business but how to keep family a priority from my dad.

I love spending time with my three sons, nine grandkids, my wife and her three daughters. We get together for meals, birthdays, parties and just to have fun. My oldest granddaughter is in cheer, so we attend a lot of games as well as all the other activities in which my grandkids are involved. On special occasions, my sons and I get together for golf. We usually play at the Moon Valley Country Club in Phoenix, but my favorite course is Cypress Point in Monterey, California.

As a father, I teach my kids the good way to live life that Proverbs 3:5-6 provides: "Trust in the Lord with all your heart and lean not on your own understanding; in all your ways acknowledge him, and he will make your paths straight." I believe that it's the Lord who sets things up, directing us to make the right moves for the unforeseen things ahead. Each experience prepares us for what follows. I remember a very difficult lawsuit we once found ourselves in with the USGA. The case enveloped my father and the stress was enormous; however, he did not lose faith. The case was finally settled, and we were able to move on; but the experience taught me a great deal, especially how to prepare for tough situations. Someone once made a comment about us, "You're a small company but act like a big one," because they respected the way we did business.

It truly is a family affair at PING. I look after the interests of our whole family because we all work together: my oldest son runs the golf clubs, my middle son takes care of soft goods, and my youngest is in charge of club fitting and education. I have a niece who looks after everything for the ladies' market, one who helps with government affairs, and a daughter who does market research. Two of my nephews work in Research/Testing and Information Systems, respectively. My oldest brother's sons-in-law are both Vice-Presidents: one oversees our legal department, and the other is responsible for our continuous improvement efforts. Everyone is highly capable, carrying their own load.

We run our business quite differently than most, because we do it for the glory of the Lord. We work very hard on our designs. My father's passion revolutionized the golf industry with his designs, and he is the only golf manufacturer in the World Golf Hall of Fame. As our mission statement says, we're "committed to being the unquestioned leader in innovation, design, service and quality while providing an enjoyable environment for employees that allows them to fulfill their potential."

We take care of our employees. This was something near to my dad's heart, and I continue to expand on it. We give our employees a wonderful retirement plan and exceptional health benefits. As a dad and the "father" of the business, I look after everyone.

As I look to the future, I think of the impact every decision has on our business; and our business is family. I love my family. I love my kids. Fatherhood is indeed the Lord's biggest gift, so it's important to me to leave this company in better shape than when my father passed it onto me, and I trust that someday, my boys will do the same with their kids. They are included in all the daily decisions. They all have so much potential. I feel proud watching them grow and succeed in their positions.

Don't let anyone tell you that being a father isn't difficult; it is, but the real joy is the wonderful glow of satisfaction you get from it. Fatherly advice for those beginning this journey- remember you are a role model for your kids, so live life the way you want your kids to live it.

J.J. – In 1994, the National Golf Foundation named the Solheims "Golf Family of the Year." Successful in business, loving in family, the Solheims inspire us all.

Today, let's make family our business and strive to see that all members feel successful in their position in it.

THE IMPORTANCE OF FAMILY

Joseph Stambouli
Lebanon

J.J. – Special thanks to Joseph Stambouli's son, Christopher, for his assistance with his father's section. I first met with Christopher in a restaurant in Orange, CA, to discuss the project with him. Excited to have his father a part of Fathers' Wisdom, he was able to connect with his father in Lebanon about the book, which prompted this touching essay about the importance of family. Later, when I needed Joseph to review the edited version of his story, Christopher flew to Lebanon so that his father could read it.

—

The political regime in Syria, my country of origin, was taking its toll on the mentality of the people and its educational system. I felt an impending urge to move to Lebanon, which enjoyed a better standard of living as well as excellent schools for my children. Because my business in Syria was lucrative, I chose to keep working there, leaving my family in Lebanon and seeing them just a few days each month, talking with them nightly by phone. I did this for seven years.

During this time my wife assumed head of the household, caring for the children's needs and education, which gave her strength and self-confidence, but she was alone in this task. After just one year in that situation, I decided to leave the children in boarding school and bring my wife to live with me. Prepa-

WISDOM FROM A STEPDAD

Darwin Bicknell
California

    When I was five years old, I had a profound experience which transformed my life. I was on my way to the store one morning when I accidentally found myself in the middle of a sticker patch. I was barefoot, and the thorny briers pierced my skin. The pain in my feet was so intense, I fell down in the patch, and stickers attacked my entire body. I lay helpless, covered with the piercing thorns. All I could do was cry. My dog was with me, but I knew he could do nothing to save me. I had to save myself. So one by one, I carefully pulled the stickers out of my skin, got on all fours and blew the thorns to the sides to make a path for my escape. The realization that I was alone in the world hit me, and I knew it was up to me to find my way through life.

    From getting myself out of this predicament, I was empowered to go forward in life knowing that God was with me, and anything was possible.

    Life was still tough. I grew up in poverty and in a neighborhood where people accepted the status quo and didn't seem to strive for more. I slowly lost the confidence that I had gained and let my circumstances get the best of me; I never graduated from high school. I also lost my faith in God and spent several years in aimless living. As the responsibilities of adulthood grew overwhelming, I reconnected with the powerful part of me that got out of that sticker patch. I focused on work and living a God-honoring life. I then bought my first home at twenty-three and started my first successful business at twenty-four.

As a grandfather, I spend the time with my grandkids that I wish I could've spent with my kids. We surf, camp, hike, and go to church together. I also plan events such as beach days and sleepovers for my kids and grandkids to give them special times to look forward to and unite as a family. My life has come full circle. I have grown from being a son, to a father, to now being a grandfather–a leader and mentor for my kids and grandkids.

I share the wisdom of all my years with my kids and grandkids. I pass on my Christian faith and tell my kids that even though their earthly father will one day be gone, their Heavenly Father will always be with them.

One of my sons found himself in tough times and had to live in a motel with his three kids for a while. He shared how upset he was about this with me. I assured him that I'd watch over him and never let him starve. I was loving enough to explain to him that this was a result of some his own choices, and he now had the opportunity to choose differently and figure his way out of the situation, which he did.

I compare all of my children to tomatoes, for no matter how well I water, prune and affirm them, not all of them will grow into robust tomatoes. I combine active parenting with quietly sitting back and letting my children grow as individuals. If parents have children who are more difficult to raise or have more problems growing up, they shouldn't fix all their attention on these children, but should give abundant love to all their kids. Hopefully, all the children will blossom, but if some don't or blossom later, whether life seems easy or difficult for them, it's important as a father to be there for all of them.

J.J. – I interviewed Darwin during a couple of phone calls between his visits to family members. True to his word, he was in the midst of keeping his commitments to them. At the end of our talk, he said, "Game on." The game he spoke of was the game of life, and his has been doubly blessed by being a father and stepfather.

Today, let's live in the spirit of "Game on!" and go forward with enthusiasm in our great game of life.

FATHERHOOD AND LIFE–IMPROV STYLE

Greg Atkins
California

I was raised in the 1960s during the golden era of growing up. My family was just like the *Leave It to Beaver* television show. My father worked a regular nine-to-five type job, came home and had dinner with my mom and me. My parents loved each other deeply and had a great relationship. I never saw them fight, and I always felt supported by them both in whatever I did. The fairytale ended when at the age of seventeen my father suddenly passed away leaving my mother and me alone. Her support for me did not fade, even in this hard time.

A year later, I made a huge decision: I wanted to be an actor. Many parents discourage their children from entering the arts, fearing that they need a more "secure" career. My mother told me that when my father was in high school, he also acted and so impressed his drama teacher, he was encouraged to go to New York and talk to an agent about a career in acting. Swayed by his own father and the lure of a "secure" career, he went to work in a gas station instead. Maybe my mother felt my dad would want me to know this.

My mother's support and faith in me paid off. I studied theater and have been fortunate enough to have a highly successful career working as an actor, writer, and director in many areas of the entertainment industry and corporate world. I have taught improvisational acting at South Coast Repertory Theatre in Costa Mesa, CA, for the past thirty-five years. I am also a published author and playwright, and my plays are produced around the world. My latest book, *IMPROV! A Handbook for the Actor*, is "a staple in the improvisation world." I currently travel extensively with my acting company, InterActors. The actors play the role of patients to help train doctors to better diagnose their patients. In the past year, I have traveled to twenty-three cities with my acting troupe. I am grateful to succeed in the arts and live my passion.

I am now a single dad and have two daughters, ages fourteen and twenty-two. Being divorced and sharing custody with my ex-wife has not hindered my commitment to my girls—I'm there for them 100% of the time that I have them. I take them to school, pick them up and help wherever I can. I am blessed to have my own business and a flexible schedule so I can spend a lot of time with my girls. Most fathers who work a nine-to-five job just have some evenings and weekend time to spend with their children. I have the luxury to change my schedule to meet my daughters' needs.

I enjoy a close, honest relationship with both my daughters. Guys tend to be more even keel, and with my daughters, I have learned to flow with their "girl drama." Our open communication style lets this happen with love and acceptance. If one of my daughters is extra emotional, she's free to tell me that she's "PMS-ing" or whatever else is going on with her. If one is quiet and not up to talking, that's okay, too. I'm safe for my daughters to share with since I'm also sensitive and emotional. I cry with them at movies, and we frequently say, "I love you," to each other.

There are times I do activities with my daughters that I don't care for, but my love for them supersedes my tastes in activities. I am not a sports fan, and one of my daughters is a song leader. In spite of my dislike for football, I attend all of her games to show her my love and support.

The activity I treasure the most with my girls is dress shopping, especially when they need a special outfit for a dance or event at school. They value my input since I know about costumes from my experience in the entertainment industry. I've gone with my daughters to buy all of their prom dresses. One day, I will be the one to help them pick out their wedding dresses.

Fun is a regular part of our family life, and having a sense of humor also helps with relationships and raising kids. My oldest daughter once told me about the time she got her first kiss. She said that when the guy leaned forward to kiss her on the cheek, she turned her head towards him, and he kissed her on the eyeball. It wasn't funny at the time, but my daughter and I later laughed over her first kiss being on her eyeball. We love to laugh together by watching shows like *Duck Dynasty* and the movie, *Elf*, and we play boards games like Yahtzee. I like inviting my daughters' boyfriends over to play games with us. I have observed a lot about a boy's character this way. I can see if the boy gets super competitive and how he treats my daughters. Games bring out the true character of a person.

One of the most hilarious things we do is celebrating made-up holidays, such as Spanksgiving, which we celebrate the week before Thanksgiving. It's our way of "slapping the turkey on the ass." Guests can bring any dish they'd like, such as salmon, a vegetarian entrée or the traditional turkey. The entrance fee to Spanksgiving is to share what one is grateful for in a creative way, such as singing a song or doing a puppet show.

Sometimes humor comes in the most precious day-to-day conversations and actions of my kids. I remember when my youngest daughter was a preteen and shyly said he had something to tell me. "Remember when I told you that I didn't like

J.J. – On the day that I interviewed Greg, he thought we were to meet at 10:00 a.m., and I thought we were to meet at 11:00 a.m.. At 10:15 a.m., Greg called and asked where I was. I told him I thought our meeting was at 11:00 a.m., and we agreed to keep that time. I felt horrible, because the last thing an interviewer wants is to be late for the interview.

When I arrived, Greg met me with a smile and said that he'd shopped at Target. It was improv in action, for he easily went to Plan B. I appreciated his spirit of grace and ability to go with the flow. In truth, life is improv all the time.

Greg is a man of humor by trade and by nature. As I reviewed my notes to write his section of the book, I smiled, being reminded to focus on life's fun and joy. True to Greg's happy spirit, his parting words to me were, "Life is supposed to be fun."

Today, let's focus on the positive, light side of life. Laugh, smile, and have fun!

HANDS-OFF / LOVE-ON FATHER

Jerry Moore, J.D.
California

When I was five years old my father was killed. It became the job of my mother, grandmother and later on, my stepfather, to raise me. I sought to develop close relationships with my own children after missing this with my own father. I have three sons, now ages fifty-one, fifty-five and fifty-seven, and eight grandchildren.

As my sons were growing up, we spent a lot of time together. We went regularly to the Colorado River to waterski and had season tickets to Dodger games. We even went to the World Series game when the Dodgers played the Oakland A's. I attended every football and soccer game they played and coached Little League for all three of my sons.

When one of my sons was young and a coach was teaching him how to swim, he told his mother, "My mind is stronger when dad is here." I felt grateful for the confidence and security he felt with me.

I am a grandfather now and support my grandchildren in their activities. I cheer them on at dance recitals, drama performances and basketball games. I get on the floor and play games, like pickup sticks. Twice, I dressed in overalls and drove the choo-choo train around the playground at one of my grandchildren's elementary school fairs.

As much as I am involved with my family, I am also a hands-off father who never micromanages them. I have a more laissez-faire approach to parenting, but my kids and grandchildren know they can depend on me when needed.

When my sons were in high school, I told them that if they got a 3.2 or higher grade point average, they could get into the University of California system. I hoped my sons would go to UCLA, and all three later graduated from there. When I attended their graduations, the depth of my joy was massive. Three grandchildren have graduated from college; Trine, Chelsea and Corbin; and Margaret is starting college in the fall. I also give my sons a sense of their specialness without overdoing it, so that they have a healthy, balanced view of themselves. I'm grateful that they're all strong, independent adults with solid values.

Two of my sons adopted children. One son adopted a girl, Dasha, who was an orphan in Siberia; and another adopted a boy, Brandon, who'd been abandoned by his mother and was dropped off at Orangewood Children's Foundation in Orange County, CA, which helps abused and neglected children. I give my adopted grandchildren extra love and attention, feeling they had a raw deal for how they began life. One time, I told Dasha, "I love you every minute, every hour, all day. I love you." An hour later, I heard her tell her sister, "Grandpa loves us all the time, every minute, every hour." She knew she was loved, the greatest blessing of all.

I am so thankful for the close relationships I have developed with my sons. I realize now that they're adults living their own lives and don't need my guidance like when they were young. I taught them more by example than by giving them advice. For instance, I showed them how to have a strong work ethic by being a good employee who works hard and does his responsibilities. Employees usually get what they deserve, so if they want to be promoted, they need to work with the expertise, positive attitude and commitment to rise in their profession. If my sons discuss issues with me, instead of telling them what to do, I remind them to take life a day at a time and that the situation will pass.

Childrearing is hard work, and especially difficult for the mother. I loved being helpful to my wife and reminding myself that it was not her child, but our child. I used to boil my sons' baby bottles and get up in the middle of the night to feed them. Fatherhood is the most satisfying thing in my life.

J.J. – Jerry ended our interview with a smile and told me how much he'd enjoyed our conversation. His smile told the truth in his heart – he's hands-off, but as his granddaughter Dasha said, he's love-on, "every minute, every hour." Fatherhood is indeed his greatest satisfaction.

Today, let's live boldly by example and take a 'hands-off' approach, giving one another the freedom to be oneself.

MY GREATEST JOY

Steven Russell
California

The moment I became a father, everything changed within me. I was self-centered and focused only on earning money, working as a recruiter in the Silicon Valley in California. Then the doctor handed me my precious first child, Jessica. I felt her life, her energy, and instantly, she became my number one priority. I had a new direction—to take care of my little girl.

With my new priority in place, we moved to a rural area in Northern California for a more peaceful and family- centered life in a safe environment; and then we had a son. Although my life's focus had turned so completely around as a father, somehow my marriage fell on rocky ground, and when my son was just five years old, our marriage ended. I was fearful that I would lose my children, but fortunately, my ex-wife and I had 50/50 custody, so I spent plenty of time with my kids.

My greatest concern was being able to support myself and my kids. Financial fears were real to me. I was working then as a career counselor in a federally funded program, not knowing if the funding would be cut. It never was, but whenever my kids stayed with me, we kept to a budget. I decided to find fun doing ordinary things, like visiting the pet store, exploring the used bookstore, going to Kmart to buy a small toy, and even having an adventure, shopping for groceries. I wanted them to enjoy being kids and have lots of time to play. I just wanted my kids to be kids.

I did not believe in punishing my children. If they made a mistake, we talked about it until they understood. Once I knew they "got it," I let them go play. This was easy for my daughter. She was intuitive and picked up things quickly. It was more difficult for my son because he had so much energy and was always on the go. We'd talk about it, but sometimes he was so amped up that I didn't really think he understood. So I would have him sit and see if he would calm down enough for him to "get it." A minute for him was like an hour for someone else. He finally learned to calm down quickly because he desperately wanted to go run and play. I saw other parents give their kids severe groundings, which seemed to just teach them to be better liars to their parents. I wanted my children to talk with me about anything. I wanted them to make mistakes while they were young so we could learn together.

Once my son hurt another boy. I wanted him to understand how the other boy had felt being hurt, so that he wouldn't do it again. We sat on the couch, and I asked him over and over, "What if that were you, how would you have felt?" I was hoping if he could understand how it felt, it would keep him from doing that again. Suddenly, he burst into tears. I just held him and let him cry. When he was done, he told me he was sorry. I knew then that he "got it."

Growing up, I was told to be tough, tough, tough; don't express your feelings. I didn't want to raise my children this way, so I encouraged them to feel their feelings. I taught them that feelings have a beginning, middle, and end, and that if they just felt them, they'd pass. Feelings are to be felt, not feared. I want my kids to feel love for themselves and to feel good about who they are.

"Trust life, for life is on our side," I often say. Life always brings us the experiences we need for our highest growth, and as long as we're learning, life is fun. Trusting life is an intellec-

MY GREATEST JOY

tual concept, but to really live its power and peace, we need to believe it at the deepest level. Doing something we regret, that's the hardest obstacle. I tell my kids it's not a cause for judgment, but that they're just given a vision of a different way to handle the situation in the future. It's a gift. Looking back at our most difficult moments, we see that through them, we grew stronger and came to a better place. We learn that life is worth trusting and that a higher power of love and wisdom guides us all.

Being a father has always come easy for me because I love being a dad. My favorite times are any times that I'm with my kids. They are my greatest joy; nothing else even comes close!

Today, let's trust life and be assured that it is on our side.

MY GREATEST GIFT

Jessica Russell, Ph.D.
California

J.J. – After I interviewed Steven Russell, I felt it would be interesting to interview his daughter, Jessica as well. I talked to them separately. Neither was aware of the questions which I asked or their respective answers. It was remarkable because when Steven told me what he wanted to teach Jessica, she stated these teachings as what she learned from him. It was harmony in mind and heart between a father and daughter connected through their bond of love.

—

I call my dad the Yoda of Life. He is a warrior who takes on life with enthusiasm and meets challenges with grace, finding the positive in what others perceive as adversity. Beyond all, he embodies this wisdom as a way of life.

One of the best gifts my father gave me was the ability to feel. When my brother and I got hurt, he comforted us, but instead of saying, "It's okay," he sat with us and listened, often just to our tears, and said, "Yeah, yeah…Wow, keep feeling it." He didn't want to say it was okay, because it wasn't. We were hurting, and he loved that we expressed those feelings. He didn't want to minimize our feelings and teach us to pretend that we were okay when we weren't. At times when I've sought direction, he's told me to just feel my feelings, and I'll know what to do next. This has worked, and I follow my intuition as a result.

Lately, I've struggled with self-love and acceptance, and he told me to surround myself with people who make me feel the absolute best. "Don't spend one second with anyone or anything that doesn't make you feel good inside. Not one second, Jessica. You're too amazing to spend time with those who make you feel less than that. Most importantly, that includes yourself; don't spend one second with those negative thoughts. Not one second. Release them and walk away."

Having a father who loves and accepts me completely is indeed my greatest gift. His acceptance, coupled with his wisdom and true joy, provide a model for life–a true Yoda. I don't always remember what my father says or does, but how he makes me feel- cherished forever.

Today, let's feel our feelings to guide us to work, people and activities that bring us joy.

THE FATHER-SON RELATIONSHIP

Erik Arnesen
California

My mother passed away when I was just two years old. My sisters and I were sent to live with other family members. Through the course of time, my family was reunited with my father. This difficult journey, the unifying force of family, especially the importance of the father-son relationship, made an incredible impact on my life.

My father had left his Norwegian homeland and sailed to Seattle, Washington, and then to California where he became an architect. I greatly revered his courage and sense of adventure for sailing and immigrating to a new country. My father's hero was Roald Amundsen, the man who led the first successful expedition to the South Pole in 1911. He gave me the middle name, Roald, in his honor.

My father taught me to "go the extra distance." On one occasion when I was a small boy, I rode with him to deliver architectural plans to a client. When I asked why we were delivering the plans instead of sending them, my father replied, "Always go the extra distance." There's a ceremonial aspect to a relationship with clients, and I always go the extra distance for them. It's a way of honoring the relationship where one's livelihood exists.

When I turned fifteen years old, my father passed away. In mourning his death, I experienced a great loss of identity. I was the youngest in my family and felt that I had lost my anchor. Later, when I married, I had a son. I was determined to have a close bond with him since I'd missed such a relationship with my father. I named my son, Ragnar, after my father. As a small child, Ragnar was diagnosed with diabetes. He has undergone two transplant surgeries, and I was his first donor. When people ask me if donating a kidney to my son made us closer, I say that it hadn't because we already were close. I taught my son the importance of being fit for his overall health and to help control his blood sugar. Physical fitness is a regular part of Ragnar's life, and he has competed numerous times in the International Transplant Games to celebrate the gift of life and raise awareness of the need for organ donors.

There was a time the closeness I share with my son stood in jeopardy. When Ragnar was five years old, my wife and I divorced. Our breakup was painful, but my ex-wife and I were determined to stay on good terms for our son's sake. "Life is too short to carry difficulties too far into the future." Thus we maintained a positive relationship which has helped to heal the past. After the divorce, I lived in San Francisco, while Ragnar lived in Sausalito with his mother. Since my relationship with my son was of the utmost importance, I frequently drove to Sausalito to see him. It was "a benefit in disguise," because this time brought us closer together. We talked as companions, and our time was "together-oriented," not "event-oriented."

I work as a photojournalist, and this has led me to travel around the world. I wanted to teach Ragnar to be skilled and comfortable as an independent traveler. I gave him many travel opportunities as he grew up and encouraged him to travel on his own. "Life is not a theory. You have to go and see it and get a hold of it. The wider your experience, the more you are in tune, curious, compassionate and able to embrace humanity." I taught Ragnar that, "Humanity is worth more than a picture of humanity." Sometimes, instead of taking a photo that might've been valuable for my work, I spent time with the people instead. For instance, one time when I walked into a South African village living under apartheid, I played with a child instead of taking a photo to show him that I, a white man, was safe. Life is not a movie set for life. Reality is more exciting than the romantic notions we carry.

I've spent my life falling out of airplanes into other people's lives, rattling across the globe like a stick on a picket fence. I get deep into its nooks and cracks, wanting to go over that next ridge and around the next corner.

I wanted a sense of the sea because my father had traveled to the U.S. by boat, so in 1993, I sailed over 3,000 miles from Cartagena, Columbia, through the Panama Canal to San Diego, CA. My father loved being alone on the ship on watch at night, and I share this same joy. I missed some business, but the experience was worth more than money, and my memories will live longer than any job I might've done.

The sea holds another joy that my son, Ragnar, and I can share. We both love to surf–the solitude of surfing and being in the moment while riding the waves. In order to catch a wave, you must paddle out to meet it. In life, you must leave the shore and paddle out to participate. Ragnar's and my motto is, "It's time to paddle out," meaning to go for it and engage in life.

Today, let's step off the shore of our comfort zone and paddle out to further our ride on the wave of life.

Note: In 2007, Ragnar's kidney/pancreas transplant rejected. In 2009, he received a kidney from his cousin, but unfortunately that rejected after only a week. Since then, Ragnar has been on continuing dialysis while he awaits yet another transplant. In that time, he has married and continues a life of rigorous athletic training and an extraordinary positive attitude that continues to astound all who know him.

3

BALANCE

"As a father, I was called on to be a
'Jack of All Trades,' but to gain mastery as a parent,
that is a lifelong task."

✣

Dick Parks

THE COACH

Richard Miller
California

I have three daughters: Melissa, Jennifer and Tori. I was their coach, protector and cheerleader. I cheered them on and gave them confidence for life by letting them know that they were always loved. I watched them grow and change and meet life with such potential, and then–I lost two of my three daughters to cancer. My daughter Tori's faith helped me deal with my loss and ultimately accept that, "What is, is." I spent time listening to my daughters, showing as much courage, confidence and strength that I could; but it was my strong belief in God that helped sustain me when my daughters were ill and how to cope, even now. My youngest daughter, Tori, who passed away said, "Life is a gift." Tori's daughter painted a large bright red heart with this saying on it in honor of her mother, and it hangs in my hallway, among family photos and other cherished mementos. I've learned to endure pain and heartache and continue on with a positive stance for, "Tomorrow is a new day."

Each of my daughters had such distinct personalities. I treated them differently based on their temperaments as well as collectively as a family. Sometimes discipline affected only one; at other times, it affected all three. I parented like a coach, and we all had input, as a team. In our family meetings, I helped my kids realize that they needed to be considerate of one another and adhere to certain standards in order to have a harmonious family unit. For instance, I told them that they needed to respect each other and give one another space when they shared the backseat of the car. We never wanted our children to be afraid to tell the truth. If one broke a dish, it was okay to admit it. Then we could deal with the issue openly and resolve it in a timely and comfortable way.

I fondly remember the year I took a sabbatical from teaching, and we all went to Japan. When we returned, we traveled across the U.S. for three months. It was in times like these that my daughters and I developed a close family relationship. I would often talk with each of them, one-on-one, about what their dreams were, what they wanted to do in the future. I would say, "Believe in yourself, set goals, and have the courage to pursue your dreams."

I enjoy the role of coach. Being a father is like being a coach. A coach teaches, trains and prepares his team for competition or other goals. A father teaches, trains and prepares his children for life. I've served in a coaching role in many positions in my life. I taught elementary, junior high and then high school where I coached swimming and water polo. I instilled confidence in my athletes through training and the repetition of skills to increase their expertise. Several of my swimmers and water polo players later became U.S. Olympians. I remember taking my oldest daughter to swim meets, encouraging her to pursue her goals and helping her plan for their attainment. I used the diagram of the "Franklin T," where a "T" is written on a piece of paper and divided into a "What" column on the left and a "Result" column on the right. The "What" column could be the goal of going to college, or whatever goal we discussed, and the right column could be the "Result" of becoming a teacher, and so on. Then the steps would be listed for what was needed for this result.

After twenty years of teaching, I became the Chief Lifeguard for Long Beach following my father and uncle who previously served in this role. I was then appointed Manager of Beaches and Marines for Long Beach. Now in retirement, I continue to serve in coaching/leadership positions such as being the Commodore for the Long Beach Yacht Club. I give my Vice and Rear Commodores assignments and the materials and knowledge to complete them. I let them do the work without micromanaging them, and I'm always open for questions to best support them in their duties. I'm also in the United States Life Saving Association and the World Life Saving Association, which trains lifeguards and promotes lifeguarding on an international level. I love the life-giving mission of being a lifeguard and the relationships I have built along the way. I recently returned from a trip with other yacht club members where we enjoyed our travels and nurtured our relationships. Once a week, I meet friends for breakfast whom I've known since elementary school. My life continues to expand as I meet new friends and enjoy the richness which such relationships bring.

As my daughter Tori said, "Life is a gift." So, I will continue to unwrap, develop and cherish the presents of my life and seek to enrich others' lives as well.

> *J.J. – I was honored to interview Richard at his home where I also met his wife and daughter Jennifer. His coaching skills in organization, planning, leadership and support were evident within the first minute of our talk. He had prepared a list of wise principles which he lives and passes on to others. After we spoke, he showed me the pictures and other mementos in their hallway, such as the vibrant red heart which Tori's daughter painted for her mother. Although Tori's earthlypresence has passed, her*

wisdom, faith and light live on through her family and her message that, "Life is a gift."

Today, let's start our day cheering each other on and end our day with thanks for our life. Let's live the day fully, and always remember that, "Life is a gift."

THE FAMILY WHEEL

Dick Parks
Hawaii

What is my purpose for being? My role as a father? I've asked myself this many times in an attempt to flush out an answer that will give me an idea, direction, or meaning of significance. I'm determined to make the most of what I've been handed in this life. I call it survival. To be a survivor, I've learned I must have goals. Without goals, life has no direction, and without direction, one rambles aimlessly, accomplishing little that lends itself to a long and quality life.

My own father's parentless childhood resulted in a troubled, orphaned life in a California Youth Authority Confinement Center and several years in San Quentin Prison. After his early release on good behavior, he met my mother, and she gave him the reasons he needed to aim his life in a positive direction. For the first time in his life, he had purpose, because he had love. Unfortunately, some of the negative traits my father learned in his unguided and unloved youth arose and at times were directed towards me.

We were a family of five: dad, mom, me, sister, and brother. Our financial status as a poultry ranching family alternated between low and low middle income. No one could outwork my father: sun-up to sundown, seven days a week. When I was in school, I was expected to do the same. He had zero tolerance for lying and cheating, and stressed respect, manners, and honesty. This was in response to his experience growing up incarcerated. He would not allow his children to replicate the lifestyle that had caused him so much pain.

Discipline was usually a profane reprimand and almost always physical. Sometimes, the physical discipline escalated into fists, feet, belts, or belt buckles. These severe measures were tied to my father's alcoholism, which I believe was brought on by endless days of labor and low income with little light in sight. He never quit trying. He just stumbled along the way.

As a young man, I swore that I'd never allow the negative influences of my father's alcoholism, lack of education, or volatile temper to be a part of me or my family's life. It's been a struggle, but I've done a reasonably good job of keeping my word to myself. Education opened my eyes to choices which I never knew existed. I was fortunate to be the only member in my family to attend college. My parents' formal education was limited to high school and below. Knowing that education was my way out of the hazy and obscure future that awaited me, I completed two majors, two minors, a Bachelors degree and a Masters degree. This gave my parents and me great pride, as a giant goal was realized.

These new influences shaped my growth and led to my wise choice of my lifelong partner and mother of our children. She has been a mainstay in helping build a proud and functional family. Where I was weak in a part of my approach to the family, my wife was strong. Where she was weak, I was strong. Balance and consistency was our answer. The sum of what I am culminates from my life experiences. My strength as a man, husband, father, leader, follower, protector, provider, friend, or if necessary a foe, is enhanced by the diversity of my life's challenges. I'm grateful to be a father, proud of my children; and I hope that I'm a good, even great, father for them. Being a father is not easy. But then the most valuable things in life never are easy.

THE FAMILY WHEEL

Over the years, I've amassed a number of human behaviors which I believe are the key elements for building a strong family unit. I chose the diagram of a wheel to demonstrate the strength of family, because it's mobile and strong in design with family at the center. The family must be the focal point, with each spoke (human behavior) extending out to the rim. How far out is the rim? It's infinite, because the spokes, such as love and sensitivity, are limitless. The mobile design is crucial, because as one's environment changes, the wheel and human behaviors must roll along or be left behind. The following are the spokes or infrastructure that give balance and symmetry to the Family Wheel.

- Love
- Respect
- Honesty
- Sensitivity
- Integrity
- Goal-Oriented
- Diligent
- Self-Discipline
- Jack of Many Trades and a Master of Some

I recommend that all future fathers integrate the Family Wheel into their lives. They must remember above all else, that they'll go nowhere unless it's based on the primary foundation of love. As a father, I was called on to be a Jack of All Trades, but to gain mastery as a parent is a lifelong task. I see a father as a man who provides care and protection. He's most effective if he's a trusted leader who leads by example.

What is my purpose for being? Although I don't have the complete answer, I know that being a father has blessed my life with soul-filling meaning and the most rewarding purpose.

Today, let's live the Family Wheel spoke of being Goal-Oriented and work toward a goal to help us live our life's purpose.

LOVED FOR THE "WHOLE HIM"

Terje Doresius
Norway

I define my role as a father as being a friend to my children. I remember once when my daughter had an emotional breakup with the boy she had been dating at the time, and she cried on my shoulder. I was able to share some of the experiences from my life to help comfort her. My father had been easy to talk to and available with his time, and I wanted to emulate these behaviors when I became a father. He read fairytales to me when I was young and talked with me about sports and business when I got older. I read fairytales to my son and daughter. I smile when I remember how they especially liked the stories I told them about trolls.

I prioritized time with my family and left my work in computer sales at a specific hour to come home and have dinner with them. I would only do additional work after dinner, if needed. My family got closer on holidays traveling together through Europe and spending time at our beach cottage an hour south of Oslo, Norway. I've enjoyed watching my children grow and change directions, and I've learned to accept their growing independence. When my daughter was twelve years old, she wanted to take the train with two of her cousins to our beach cottage. My wife and I first said, "No!" My daughter persisted, and we finally agreed to let her go. Later, I encouraged her to take a job as an au pair in France for one year. She became more independent as she cooked and took care of the three children, for whom she was responsible. She also taught them to ski in the Alps and became fluent in French.

I adore sports. My children were on skis as soon as they could walk, and they loved Alpine and cross-country skiing. My son was very active in ski jumping from the age of eight until he was twenty-two. I took him to sports clubs to train and to his competitions. I also sent him to a private ski gymnasium for his education. I golfed with my son, and we often played three generations together with my wife and father. My daughter did gymnastics, tap dancing and jazz- ballet. She also became a Telemark ski instructor. Although I loved to be involved with my children in sports, I didn't push them but let them participate in the activities they chose for the time they desired.

J.J. – Terje's son, Morten, then commented, "My father is good all the way through. He was there for my sister and me, and we felt supported by him growing up. I appreciated talking to him about various matters, and we now discuss work. What I like most about my father is—the whole him!"

To be loved and respected as a father for "the whole him" is the greatest compliment a parent could receive.

Today, let's accept and value "the whole him or her" of others and ourselves.

GOODBYE WORKAHOLISM, HELLO FAMILY

Rodric Rhodes, Ph.D.
California

My father is a caring, compassionate, and empathetic man who taught me to be open-minded, nonjudgmental, and to treat others with respect. As an educator, psychologist, and U.S. Equestrian Federation Steward, he led a busy professional life. He traveled around the country, stewarding equestrian competitions, which left little time to spend with me.

I remember going on a hiking trip with my Boy Scout troop to Bear Ridge in the Sierra Nevada Mountains. Other fathers joined their sons on the trip, and I wished my father was there to encourage me on the hike and cheer for me when I finished it. I do remember a time when my father spent the entire day with me, doing whatever I wanted to do that day. We went go-karting and to an IHOP restaurant. He ventured out of his comfort zone to give me this special day, and it meant a lot to me.

My father's academic and professional accomplishments have inspired me to pursue education. I have earned two doctorates and have a successful practice as a Licensed Clinical Psychologist and Social Worker.

I am now the father of two sons—one who is six years old and another who just turned one. When I became a father, my wife and I chose for me to be our family's sole provider. I felt driven in my work to ensure that our financial needs were met. I took these behaviors to an extreme, much like my own father, and spent little time with my family. I knew the pain of not having that father connection, so I changed my work schedule. I cut back on some late nights and weekend work. I volunteered to be a referee in my six-year-old son's soccer league and attend all my son's practices and games. I book these activities as appointments and treat them just as I would my professional appointments.

It's important for me to spend both a quantity and quality of time with my family, where my attention is fully focused on them. Once a week after soccer practice, my eldest son and I go out for a special one-on-one dinner. We shop together to choose sodas, chips, and candy for our kitchen's beverage center. Since my youngest son is an infant, I enjoy holding him and playing with him on the floor. These times are meditative to me.

I want my children to know I support them in every area. I cheer for my eldest son so often he now just smiles and bashfully replies, "I know dad. I know I did good." I also support my children by providing them with structure and discipline to keep commitments and follow rules. My eldest son may want to finish a video game when it's time to go to bed. I empathize with his disappointment, but I count "one-two-three" and then have a consequence if he doesn't transition to the next activity.

I teach my sons to be kind and giving to others and to be grateful for all that they have. I also want them to know that it's okay to be vulnerable and admit their mistakes. I lead by example. If I feel that I need to make an amends, I do. For instance, my eldest son is reluctant to try new foods. I used to push new foods on him and insist that he finish them. This was stressful for my son, so I stopped. I apologized to him and changed from a controlling stance to gently asking him to try some of the new food before eating what he knows he likes. This change restored peace and pleasure to our meals.

It's fascinating to watch my boys' different talents emerge and develop. My children are pure sweetness. My eldest son is very kind and thoughtful. He excels in academic, creative and athletic skills. I'm also enamored with my children's appearance, and I just love looking at them!

I want to encourage all fathers to extend grace to themselves in the process of becoming a good father. My journey to become less work driven has been challenging for me. I've worked diligently to change this pattern and have been rewarded with deeper family bonds. My father is now retired from education and spends more time with our family. Both he and I are grateful for our closer connection.

Fatherhood is wonderful and challenging… Definitely a learning experience. It's the most meaningful thing I've ever experienced in my life. I love being a father. I love my sons.

J.J. – I was later privileged to visit Rod and his eldest son, James, at their home and see this love in action. James said that his favorite thing to do with his father is to play with him. He first showed me the places where they play, such as the basketball court where they shoot hoops and the patio where they play scavenger hunt. We then went inside, and he showed me his elf from the book, Elf on the Shelf. According to the story, the elf returns to the North Pole each evening, and then shows up the next day in different places in the child's home. One night, the elf put a Christmas tree in James' bedroom and decorated it. When Rod asked James how the elf traveled between the North Pole and their home so quickly, James thought a moment and responded, "He must've taken a plane." In the magical world of children, everything is possible. Next, we ventured into James' playroom. Legos, his most prized toys, covered the floor. James said that if he could spend a whole day with his father, he'd play Legos and other games with him.

When I asked James if he had anything else to tell me about his father, he said, "I love him a lot." I then told James that when I interviewed his father, he said that he loves you a lot, too! James then looked up at his father with wide, eager eyes and asked, "Really?" Rod smiled, looked lovingly at his son, and replied, "Really." James then smiled, feeling his father's special love, for no matter what age we are, nothing in life compares to the joy of loving and being loved.

Today, let's spend focused, uninterrupted time with those we love and thank them for the joy they bring to our lives.

FOOTBALL TO FATHERHOOD

Thomas Lewis
Arizona

J.J. – When I first spoke to Thomas, he was working out at the gym. It was so apropos that this former college and NFL football superstar was still keeping himself in shape. I felt a little nervous; after all he did play for the New York Giants! I was just a girl from Long Beach who had a heart to celebrate fathers and had reached out to this great athlete after a friend referred me. But after I talked with Thomas for two hours, I was in awe of his honesty, openness and caring for his daughters. What I learned in our interview was that his greatest prowess and joy lay not on the football field but in fatherhood and in his commitment to work hard and sacrifice for his family. So as we cheer on the pros, ought we not cheer on the fathers? Go Team—Team Family—the best team of all!

—

My stepfather had a tremendous impact on my life; but it was his unexpected death that propelled me to where I am today. My parents divorced when I was only a year old, and my stepfather was the only father I knew until I was older and got to know my biological father better. My stepfather was a pastor and had taught me that Christ was my personal Savior. I resisted his teaching because I had many questions about religion. I later came to accept this truth for myself, and my faith has been the foundation of my life ever since.

My stepfather told me that everyone is blessed with a gift, and that it's up to each of us to find out what it is and mature it to its fullest potential. I knew my gift was in athletics, and as an eight-year-old all the way through high school, I played football.

I fully expected to continue playing when I attended Indiana University, but due my poor grades and low test scores in high school and the enactment of the NCAA Proposition 48, I was ineligible to play my first year. I had nothing now but my studies to occupy my time. I wrote my stepfather a letter. I told him that I would never put myself in that same spot again, where someone else could control my destiny.

The following year I was eligible to play. I had difficulty, however, getting along with the coaches and just wanted to go home. My stepfather, mother and young nephew came to visit me. It was Friday night before my game, and my stepfather had a talk with me. "Listen," he said. "I'm not going to always be here for you. Your brother is in jail, and your nephew needs a father. You need to be that father figure for him. Even though you're having trials, remember you said that you would never let others control your destiny. You need to buckle down, and be a man. Men in life do not quit; they find a way around obstacles and work through them." I cried through his speech, but it changed my life. It turned on a switch, and I was able to push through and persevere.

The next day, he watched my game, and then returned to Ohio to preach. He died that night. He must've felt that his time was coming, and that was why he gave me his final bit of fatherly wisdom.

Life was hard for my mom and nephew then. My stepfather did not have life insurance, and they were both left in impoverished conditions. I was already driven, but now I had a mission—to help my mother and nephew. That year, I played my heart out. On one of my wristbands I wrote the word, "Touchdowns," and on my other wristband, my stepfather's initials. I dedicated that season to him and had my best season ever. I led the nation in punt returns. I was an All-American and led the NCAA in yardage-gained in the last three games of the season.

In 1994, I was the first-round draft pick for the New York Giants, and I headed off to New York. Thanks to the money I earned from my new position, I was able to pay off my mother's house and provide for her and my nephew. It was a blessing. I was also six credit hours from graduating when I was drafted, so I finished the credits and graduated. I was the first in my family to go to college and graduate.

From 1994 to 1997, I played for the New York Giants, and then in 1998, I went on to play for the Chicago Bears. During that time, I married my wife, and in 1998, our first daughter together, Destiny, was born. My wife had a daughter, Shelby, who was just a year and half old when I married her, and in 2001, our daughter, Lexy, was born.

During the first five years of my daughters' lives, I had little interaction with them. I was focused on working and providing for them. I did, however, love putting my daughters to bed at night. They called me, "Baby Whisperer," because I could whisper them to sleep within a few minutes.

Careers in professional sports can be short, so I eventually found work in the financial industry and traveled a lot. Since I was a guy with three daughters, I figured that their mother would be a stronger influence on them. My wife's father had not been there for her growing up though, and she helped me understand the importance of having a father at home. I learned what I was missing with my daughters and what they were missing with me. I quit that job and found work again in sports, which I loved, and where I could be at home more with my kids.

I do everything with my daughters! I take them to school and pick them up. I take them to volleyball practice and to all their games. I'm with them all the time during the week and on weekends. I love the talks we have on our drives to and from school.

Recently, I was driving my youngest daughter to school, and I asked her about her grades. She said that they were good, but she didn't sound happy about it. "That's a good thing, isn't it?" I replied. She said that the kids at school call her smart. It was okay for the kids to say she was a talented athlete, but she didn't want the reputation of being smart. I told her what my stepdad told me, "that everybody in life has been given a gift and that it's up to us to work hard and mature it to its full potential," I told her that she had been blessed with athletic ability *and* intelligence. My daughter wants to go to the Olympics in volleyball. I asked her, "If a coach wants to recruit a new player and is choosing between two of equal athletic ability, but one has a 2.8 GPA and the other has a 3.7 GPA, which one do you think the coach would choose?"

She replied, "The one with the higher GPA." She suddenly beamed with pride and told me she'd gotten a 95 on her science test the day before.

Like my stepfather, I teach my daughters about God. They have all accepted the Christian faith, but I didn't press this on them; I let them make their own choice. I've sought to teach them spiritual principles and strong ethics so that they can make responsible decisions when I am not there. I tell them that they're valuable. I want them to have an inner confidence and command respect.

My greatest challenge as a father is dealing with all the secular influences in the world: the media and my daughters' friends and teachers. I have found that for girls, self-esteem is a key issue especially in the teen years. My two older daughters are of dating age, and I've taught them that men need to open doors for them. If they go out on a date, I expect their date to meet me before he takes them out and to treat them the same way that I would treat them. My daughters say that this is old-fashioned, but recently, my fifteen-year- old daughter told me that she was talking to a guy at school about my request to meet her dates, and she said that if the guy really cared about her, he would want to do that. I was so proud of her for knowing how valuable she is as a woman.

My youngest daughter had some challenges recently with a teammate who was being pessimistic about a volleyball game they were about to play at a national tournament. I gave her a pep talk to help her shift back to her excitement about the game and to play her best. The game didn't go as she'd hoped. Later though, she told me about an assignment she had where the teacher asked the students to write about a hero. She wrote about me. She mentioned the volleyball game and that the counsel I gave her had made her a better friend and teammate. I was amazed. As a parent, I don't always know if what I'm saying makes a difference, but I learned that day, it does.

The thrills of being a college football player and professional athlete pale in comparison to the joys of being a father. My background in sports gave me a taste of the harmony and success that a united team can achieve. Now my team is my family, and no touchdown, no national record, and no miraculous catch can compete with the satisfaction of being a dad. I love my daughters. I love my wife. They are my greatest joy–my best and favorite team ever!

__Today, let's remember that our family is our team and take actions for the greatest good of all.__

4

FAITH

"I teach my sons to talk to
God in a spontaneous way, not in a
'three-piece suit' sort of way."

✢

Stanley Mutunga, Ph.D.

AN ARTIST'S VIEW OF FATHERHOOD

Robert Senske
California

My father is an eternal optimist who's always upbeat and positive. He's never in a bad mood and has faith that everything will work out fine. Once he decided to take our family to Catalina on our boat. That day, eighty mile per hour winds were expected, but he optimistically had us set sail thinking we could make it to Catalina before the storm hit. Unfortunately we didn't make it and were severely blown off course.

We shipwrecked at Camp Fox in Catalina and had to be rescued! Our treacherous journey had a happy ending though, for we had a warm vacation in Catalina, met the guests at the camp, and celebrated Easter with them. Everything did work out fine–thankfully!

I am my father's son, for I'm also an eternal optimist. I have a son and daughter who are four-and-a-half-year-old twins. I now pass on my optimism to them. I grew up at the beach and live in an oceanfront home. Swimming, sailing, and participating in other beach activities have been a dominant part of my life. I just love the beach!

My children are now learning to swim. At first, they were afraid of the water and of putting their head underwater. I told them that they didn't need to be afraid and that they could put their head underwater and hold their breath. I said, "Trust me. The ocean is our friend. It is safe." My kids now jump in the water, take big arm strokes, and hold their head underwater.

My wife and I didn't plan to have kids, but after receiving financial gifts from our mothers, we were gifted with twins through in vitro fertilization. It is so much fun to watch them grow in every area. My son recently asked why it was easier to make sandcastles out of wet sand than dry sand. I told him that water was needed to hold the sand together in the castle. When telling my daughter about our Christian faith and what I believe, I showed her a picture and said, "There are three persons of God: Father, Son, and Holy Spirit."

My daughter then questioned, "Is Jesus the oldest since he has a beard?" I had to smile at her youthful logic and was impressed with her perspective of seeing the beard as a sign of age.

When my children were born, I was reborn. They remind me of the simple joys of my youth, such as kicking my feet through the incoming waves. Fatherhood has also changed me from being selfish to selfless. My life is now focused on giving to my family. I am an artist and teach a free class to fifth-graders called, Tracing for Self-esteem. My kids also attend the course. In this class, students trace pictures and learn that they can draw things which they couldn't do otherwise. For an upcoming lesson, I told the students to bring in a picture of a hero to trace such as an avenger or Disney character. I give them tracing paper and let them trace with ink, charcoal, pastel, or watercolor. The students' self-esteem rises as they create beautiful replicas of models in their own style.

I first pursued art as an avocation, and then after graduating with a degree in political science and working in marketing, I quit my secure job and became a full-time artist. I never had any formal artistic training, but my optimism and drive, which I inherited from my father, propelled me to switch careers. I was fortunate to become one of the top maritime artists on the West Coast, and my paintings reflect my love of the beach and optimistic spirit. I paint the joy, beauty, and tranquility of the coast which I've enjoyed since being a child.

Since my family lives at the ocean, the beach is my children's playground and lab for learning and adventure. My kids like to look out on the ocean from the water's edge, play in the whitewash, sit on the lifeguard stations, and dig in the sand for shells. It's important for them to have this time away from the computer where they use their tactile senses, have their feet on the ground, and physically touch and interact with nature as they walk and feel the sand between their toes.

As a parent and artist, I see similarities between these roles. My kids and the painting on my canvas are both works in progress. I don't view my parenting choices as mistakes but as happy surprises. There are also no mistakes in my paintings, because an unintended brushstroke can lead the painting in a better direction.

In painting, I follow my intuition and let the paint and emerging picture be my guides. As a parent, I respond to my children's reactions, and their interactions are like an artistic exchange between parent and child. I follow my muse in art, and my children are now my muse. Although I provide guidance, I follow their lead before applying another brushstroke of parenting, and they become my greatest work of art.

Fatherhood has changed my life profoundly. I used to handle disappointment with stress and anger which I took out on others. I frequently drank to relieve the stress of life. I consider myself to be the spiritual leader of my family who provides the moral compass. They count on me. I stopped drinking one-and-a-half years ago and entered a new life stage committed to health and a deep spiritual faith. Through these inner and outer shifts, I became more patient, peaceful and accepting of life. I run ten miles a week at the beach and take better care of myself.

I teach my kids to handle life's disappointments in a healthier way. When my kids argue, I intervene to show them how to be kind and loving to one another. One time, I accidentally erased a feature-length episode of *Iron Man* on a DVD, and my son threw a fit. I told my son that I didn't intend to erase it, but now there was space on the DVD to record new shows. I asked him what he'd like to record instead, and we recorded five *SpongeBob SquarePants* shows. In place of one show, he gained five, and the final outcome was better than the first. Disappointment creates opportunity, a breakthrough to a better conclusion.

In 2013, I painted my image of fatherhood in a gift for my daughter entitled, *It's a Father Daughter Thing*. I usually paint one to two paintings a year, which are commissioned for thousands of dollars each. My love for my children is a greater motivator than any paycheck though. I painted this out of my joy and pure love for my daughter.

The painting shows John F. Kennedy and his young daughter Caroline in the presidential yacht, Honey Fitz. The president gazes at his small child with a look of delight in their time spent together. The painting encapsulates my love for my daughter, the ocean, my admiration for Kennedy, and passion for history. Kennedy felt safe on the boat and his beloved ocean. It was his refuge from the political tension and ever-present media on the mainland. Like Kennedy, I feel safest at sea. I imagine that in the 360° circle of life, if I turn my back on the ocean, half my problems lay behind. I can manage the ones in view, and then turn and handle the ones behind me. Just as waves rise and tower high, then break and fizzle out, life problems can loom large, and then as they're handled, life becomes peaceful, and worries wash back to sea and disappear into the giant ocean depths.

Before having children, I was like a planet, which reflected the light of other mentors. Now that I pass on my talents and serve my family and community, I'm like a star which shines its light onto others. As I pass my joy onto my children, they pass it onto others.

One time, we attended a memorial service amongst a solemn crowd. After the pastor read the final verse of Psalm 23, "Surely… I will dwell in the house of the Lord forever," (Psalm 23:6) my son exclaimed, "Amen!" Suddenly, everyone laughed at his innocent outburst. He added joy to the occasion and reminded everyone that although they were grieving, they could celebrate that the deceased now lived peacefully in the life beyond, and that vital life continues on earth, as reflected in my son's enthusiasm.

My paintings have also brought joy to others, but my children captivate my heart most of all. They are my new masterpiece.

Today, let's honor all children for the priceless treasures they are.

FATHERHOOD IS SACRED

J.R. Estrella
California

I grew up in Guadalupe, Arizona, where my mother and father made a living as migrant farm workers. During the picking season, they traveled throughout Southern and Northern California and in their absence, I lived with and was raised by my maternal grandmother. She taught me the Yaqui language, history of our tribe, and the cultural roles of men and women in Yaqui society. I am an enrolled member of the Pascua Yaqui Tribe of Arizona. Pasqua means Easter in the Yaqui language and is part of our tribe's name because we are closely related, through Catholicism, with Easter (our religion is a combination of Catholic and Native American practices). It was my grandfather who taught me the importance and responsibility of being a father. A father's main duty is to protect and care for his family.

I am proud to be the father of three adult children and four grandchildren. No matter how old my kids are, I will be a responsible and caring father until the day I die. They can always look to me for help, protection, and guidance. I lead by being an example of a diligent worker and responsible family man, and my children have grown up to be successful, responsible adults. All have earned a Master's Degree in Counseling and hold responsible positions.

My wife and I are our children's biggest supporters, counselors, and safety net. When my kids grew up, I taught them to be kind, generous and respectful. I enjoyed seeing them grow and develop, and I always encouraged them to learn about other people and cultures. My children participated in many school, sports and community activities. My wife and I constantly strive to assist our family in any way possible, in order for them to continue to prosper, be happy and healthy, and have strong, united families.

One thing that is crucial to me is passing my Yaqui Indian heritage onto my children and grandchildren. Our family travels to Guadelupe for tribal ceremonies during the year. The biggest ceremony lasts for thirty days during the season of Lent. On Easter Sunday, the dancers play different roles to reenact the crucifixion and resurrection of Christ. We participate in Talking Circles, where friends gather round a fire and talk about their families, lives, and current events. My children and grandchildren love to attend Pow Wows, where Native Americans gather to "dance, sing, socialize and honor Indian culture."[1] My son continues the legacy of our Yaqui heritage through his work as a family counselor for the Southern California Indian Center (SCIC). The SCIC promotes "social, education and economic self-sufficiency" for Native Americans in Orange and Los Angeles Counties.

Near and dear to my heart is a class I teach at the Indian Center entitled "Fatherhood is Sacred." The course was developed by the Native American Fatherhood and Families Association (NAFFA). The Arizona-based organization was founded in 2002 to strengthen "Native American families through responsible fatherhood." The organization later added a "Motherhood is Sacred" course, for they believe that, "there is no work more important than fatherhood and motherhood." Native American fathers from all tribes attend and learn the love, wisdom, integrity and discipline of fatherhood. The course approach is based on a "culturally rich model that inspires and motivates fathers

[1] www.IndianCenter.org

and mothers to devote their best efforts in teaching and raising children to develop their potential and the attributes needed for success in life."

My hope is that all fathers would nurture their children, hold them constantly, and tell them how much they mean to them and how much they are loved every day. Love is not just hugs and kisses, but also actions. Honoring and respecting the children's mother demonstrates this. The father who openly shows love and respect for the mother every day, in every way possible, demonstrates the sacredness of parenthood. My wife and I are best friends, and are our children and grandchildren's best friends and confidants. We encourage them to tell us anything; this can only happen if there is trust and unconditional love among us.

I had no books telling me how to be a dad, and I stumbled and learned along the way. It's been a fulfilling experience, and out of my gratitude for being a father, I help other Native American fathers live the divinity, responsibility and holy calling of fatherhood. My wife, Phyllis, and I celebrated fifty years of marriage on September 14, 2013.

Today, tomorrow, and for the rest of our lives, let's reflect on the sacredness and importance of our families. By honoring and respecting these sacred traditions, we honor those who have come before us and lead our lives by example for those who will follow us.

"GOD IS MY GUIDE"

Stanley Mutunga, Ph.D.
Kenya/California

I was born in Nairobi, Kenya, and grew up in the small town of Machakos. My father served as a lay preacher in the British Army there. He was an extremely formal man, and although he taught me to leave whatever I touched better than I found it, such as my room, which was good, I was determined not to be so formal. I learned that building relationships is vital, especially when working with people to complete a task.

In Kenya, I followed my father's calling and became a minister, and went on to become an evangelist and university administrator. I had a strong desire to bring people together as a community and plant churches in my home country, Kenya. Building bonds and touching lives through relationships with a positive imprint is what is most important.

In 1998, I came to the United States to teach and then became a university dean. I have three sons, and my priority is to be their father and friend and foster open communication with them. I focus on being consistent, open to listen, and spending time with each one of them informally. I teach my sons to talk to God in a spontaneous way, not in a "three-piece suit" sort of way. Each night before bed, my family gathers for prayer, and either one or all speak. Last night, I felt great pleasure as my eldest son led prayer in the intimate, detailed way I had taught him.

I see my role as the head of the family as a calling. I apply the teamwork approach at home and enjoy a happy marriage with my wife. All of my kids have different personalities and interests. I honor their individuality and help them realize their goals. I focus on God's wisdom to model and teach values and morals, and to provide guidance for my kids. The pace of life in California is fast and hectic compared to that in Kenya, and sometimes the quality of relationships suffers as a result. I balance my career and family by not taking work home. It can be challenging to sort through distractions in order to focus on developing relationships.

Following my father's advice to leave things better than they were before touching them, I do nonprofit work to help the millions of AIDS victims in Africa. I believe that God has brought me to California to get contacts and resources to assist the overwhelming numbers needing help in Africa, and I've teamed with several churches to support this mission. Together, we help provide for their basic needs such as food, schooling, supplies, medical health and leadership. I want my children to see my example and leave this world better than it was before touching it.

Today, let's have a positive impact on whatever we touch, be it a thing, person, or project and leave this world better than we found it.

J.J – As I listened to Dr. Mutunga, I was in awe of his commitment to humanity, all led by his focus on God's wisdom. He saw the plight in Africa, took action, and works to rectify it in a practical way. At the end of our interview at his Hope International University office, he gave me a book entitled God So Loves the City, in which he had written an article. He then walked me out and pushed the elevator button for me. I was humbled by his kindness and later cried reflecting upon the details which he shared with me about the AIDS tragedy in Africa. He indeed lives the counsel of his father, for he left a positive imprint on my life and has inspired me to contribute to humanity however I can.

FAITH IN ACTION

Dr. William Marmion, Ph.D.
California

One of the greatest challenges I had as a father came when my second daughter, Susie, was born prematurely with multiple health issues. We thought our child was born healthy and normal, but when we brought her home from the hospital, we discovered she was slow in motor development. When she was finally able to walk, she was destructive and broke things like our phone. We later learned she was totally deaf, retarded and autistic due to brain damage she suffered during the first twenty-four hours of her life. When Susie was just three and a half years old, my wife and I faced the heartbreaking decision that we needed more help for her than we could provide at home. We prayed and also realized that for the sake of our other children, Susie would live in state hospitals.

My wife and I have worked very hard at having a balanced life, and a part of our balance is that we are deeply involved with Susie, and though very committed to her, we would not let our concerns affect our marriage or the attention we gave to our other children. We never forced her brother or sisters to visit her, but they always went and still go to see her. Going to the state hospitals brought us into contact with other special needs children, their parents and the professional staff at the hospital. I believe my children have become more compassionate and understanding through this, of the needs of others with problems.

We are all so proud of who Susie is and of her accomplishments. She is very visually focused and strong, and she can put a

500-piece puzzle together faster than anyone in my family! She also bowls and has thrown the shot put at the Special Olympics. Susie now lives in a community home in Burbank, where she does quite well. She was baptized and then confirmed in the Catholic Church. The Bishop who confirmed her said that people like Susie are "priceless treasures" in the eyes of God. They're comparable to coins and stamps with defects because they are unique, and no price can be put upon them. My wife and I realized that our daughter is such a precious gem. She has brought out the love and concern from our friends and extended family.

As the leader of my family, I always had to juxtapose what was going on in my career with my family. I worked in education, and my family moved a lot when I changed jobs and went to graduate school for my master's and doctoral degrees. My eldest daughter was the most affected by the moves because she was in and out of different schools, which made it difficult to make and keep friends. I first taught school and later went into administration at the district level. I'm grateful for the opportunities I had in my career and know that God blessed me with them. I made my career and educational decisions believing that they were the best at the time. Overtime, I learned the importance of having a balanced life, and the only thing I would have done differently was to go more gradually with my graduate studies so as to spend more time with my precious family.

Tragedy struck again when at the young age of forty my oldest daughter, Mary Anne, passed away. I was God's instrument for my daughter's birth, and I expected her

journey on earth to last longer than mine. This was the hardest thing I've ever faced. Without my faith in God, my sorrow and pain would have been unbearable. Two years passed before I began to feel somewhat normal. If I didn't have my faith and the grace of God, I would have gone crazy. Some families never discuss the person who died. My family talks about Mary Anne and has her picture displayed. She loved life, and we want to remember her for that. I'd like an answer as to, "Why my Mary Anne?" but only God has the answer, and for now, I can accept that her death is part of life's mystery.

Having a spiritual foundation has been a primary bond in my family. When I grew up though, my family had little spiritual life. We did not go to church or even own a Bible. I remember being on my paper route when I was about eleven and having discussions with God about life and relationships. I knew that I was being guided spiritually and had more of a spiritual interest than some of my friends. When I spoke about my faith, I think I irritated some of them, but I wanted to talk about what I loved. I later learned about readiness and the concept of the "ripe banana" where people only want to eat ripe bananas and not green ones. Everyone has their own clock, and people arrive at answers to the verities of life in their own way and time, usually after great tragedy or joy. My mother was raised Catholic and then left the Church. She later returned to the Church after my father passed away.

Having faith and a spiritual life are of primary importance in my life. A spiritual view of life keeps everything in perspective so that one isn't driven by the world's values of greed, power, manipulating others, or the accumulation of money or titles. I pray and meditate daily on an individual basis and regularly with my Catholic faith community at Mass.

I taught my children to always say grace before meals. Everyone had the opportunity during this time to say an improvised prayer. My wife and I would go into their bedrooms for prayer before they went to sleep each night and ask them how their day went and what they were thinking about for tomorrow. We problem-solved and troubleshooted depending upon what our children said. We would end with a prayer like, Our Father or Hail Mary, or a special prayer for their needs and circumstances.

I believe that the greatest wisdom a person can learn is to know that he or she is a creature of God, to trust God and accept God's unqualified love. Even though our goal is holiness, and as humans we will never attain that perfectly on earth, we are made in God's image and should not devalue ourselves as "only human." From this place of valuing ourselves, we need to serve God and others. We each have a unique personality and genetic structure and can give from our talents and experiences.

J.J. – Bill then shared his spiritual insight to help me cope with a recent job loss. When I told him that I felt devastated and rejected, he said that it's important to know that I have value and to accept and use the gifts I've been given to serve God and my fellows. I could use the extra time to interview fathers for this book. Perhaps I was let go from that job so I could do another–collect and share fathers' wisdom with others.

Bill asked, "Do you need a hug?"

"Yes," I replied and was comforted by his support. Wise fathers are attuned to the needs of others, and I was grateful for the simple yet healing gesture of a father's wisdom. I left the interview feeling at peace, energized and full of hope thanks to Bill's spiritual wisdom, kindness and sensitivity.

FAITH IN ACTION

Today, let's look at our lives through spiritual eyes and feel the peace from trusting, despite the challenges and unanswered questions we face, the higher being who created us and the grand plan for our lives.

PAPA DON

Don Sprenger
California

J.J. – I interviewed Don while sitting outside a coffee shop in Seal Beach, CA. He had just returned from Maui and wore a Hawaiian shirt. This energetic eighty-year-old was so filled with joy that he smiled throughout our entire interview, which lasted almost four hours. Knowing Don, he is probably still smiling!

—

I was born in 1933, the sixth of ten children. My father was a landscaper who worked at a nursery owned by a Japanese man. After the bombing of Pearl Harbor, the owner of the nursery was forced to leave his business and was placed in an internment camp. He knew my father was an ethical man, so just before he left he offered to sell the nursery to him. My father accepted.

I began to work for my father at the nursery after school and all day on Saturdays when I was about nine years old. He taught me to be honest, have integrity and work hard. My father closed the shop on Sundays for us to rest. "If we were open seven days a week, we might seem money-hungry," he said. "We'll just teach people to buy on Saturdays," and Saturdays were huge. No matter how busy my father was though, he always made time for family; family was first.

My mother influenced me greatly. I can still see her sitting in the living room just before dawn each day. I would wander in and sit on her lap as she read the Bible and prayed for me. She introduced me to God's Word—the greatest source of wisdom. My mother passed her deep Christian faith onto me, and since then God has been the center and guiding force in my life.

I never realized how poor my family was while growing up. Maybe it was because my parents gave me so much love. Whenever you walked into our home, you were always hugged and fed. When I became a father of a son and daughter of my own, we hugged a lot, too. I now have five grandsons and three great-grandchildren, and our family's love and hugs continue.

Professionally, I worked as a fireman and was away from my family a few days a week. I then spent a lot of time with them when I was home. I worked for over thirty years for the Los Angeles Fire Department, retiring as a Captain. My son followed suit and worked at the Long Beach Fire Department where he is now a Captain. When I visit him at his station, all the firemen line up for hugs; they know we're a hugging family.

Aside from just hugs, I spent time each night with my kids as they were growing up, loving on them, praying for them, massaging their feet and giving them back rubs. They never complained about going to bed! During these times, they opened up to me about any struggles they faced. My son didn't always say much, but we connected in the silence. I told him that no matter what he did, I would always love him. It's the best feeling in the world for kids to know, "My dad loves me." When people know that they're loved, they feel secure. Kids don't always get that from their father, and I wanted to give it to mine.

One time, when my son was in junior high, he forgot to take his lunch and book bag to school. He called to ask if I could bring these to him. When I pulled up in my pickup truck, he dove through the window and hugged me in front of all his friends. Since many adolescents don't even want to be seen with their parents at school, I thought, "That is one secure kid."

When my daughter was a teen she loved horses, so I decided to buy two of them. We often spent time riding them bareback along the beach. My son and I surfed, swam and hiked together. When he was twelve, we studied the book of Proverbs. Since this Biblical book of wisdom has thirty-one chapters, we read and discussed a chapter a day for a month. As we read, we asked ourselves, "What does it take to be a wise young man?" We learned and grew together in this special time.

I have learned that the greatest gift I can give to people is my time. The older I get, the more I realize this. I volunteer my time to mentor many young men in my church's youth group. Recently, the father of a young man I've been mentoring thanked me for spending time with his son. He rarely sees him because he is so busy. I told the father, "You missed the boat. He'd love to have this time with you. Children grow and the years go by; that time is lost forever."

In order to use my time wisely, I live by priorities. We either live by pressure or by priorities. My first priority is to keep my vertical relationship right with God. That puts all my horizontal relationships right with my family, friends and business. When I worked at the fire department, I got up at about 5:00 a.m. to read my Bible. I wrote one thing I learned or a verse on a 3 x 5 card and stuck it in my pocket. I referred to it throughout the day, integrating its wisdom into my life in a practical way.

Now that I'm retired from the fire department, I still start every day with quiet time with God. I don't get involved with the television, newspaper or anything else until I'm on track with God. I tell God, "I am available. Use me, anytime."

I love to encourage others by making their day special. One time, I stopped at a gas station, and after pumping my gas, I bought the cashier a drink. I told him, "It looks like you need a cold drink." He smiled and said, "God bless you." It takes so little to make someone's day special, and it's so worth it.

Another time when three of my grandsons were little, I took them to BJ's Pizza to bring their favorite server, Patty, a rose. As the boys walked in and headed over to her with the flower, the whole restaurant got quiet. They offered her the rose, and she knelt down on her knees and hugged them. Everyone clapped. Patty and my grandsons will never forget that special day.

Several years ago, my family faced a huge challenge when my wife was diagnosed with a brain tumor. Because of this her memory is not what it used to be. Recently when we were eating out, she asked me, "What do I usually get? How do I like it?" We laughed about the situation and then enjoyed our meal. I can choose to be thankful or angry when tough things happen in life. I'd rather be happy and see my wife through God's eyes. When people ask me how she's doing, I focus on what she can do and not on her limitations. My daughter has moved in with us to help take care of her mother. This has brought them closer together. God can work good out of anything.

Five years ago, I fell off a ladder at our resort in Maui while repairing a TV antenna. When I fell, I couldn't move and lay in a pool of blood. I nearly became a paraplegic, but I regained my health, and my recovery time was a gift. My whole family visited me from the mainland, and I had more quiet time with God than I'd had in years. It was a detour for me; but God was still in control.

My life has been so filled with blessings, and being a father has been one of the greatest. What's my favorite thing about it? Everything! I adore my kids. It's the most important job I've ever had, more important than any career, or anything else. I passed on the love I was given, and now I see my kids love the Lord and love their kids. The blessing of family love continues.

***Today, let's tell God we're available and
serve the world as he directs.***

J.J. – At the end of our interview, I asked Don if he had any other comments he'd like to share about being a father. He replied, "How many days do you have?" He had told me many stories of love, and I knew that if we kept talking, I would hear still more. Eighty years of love, and he's still going strong!

That night, when I lay down for bed, I was still smiling and filled with joy from our talk. Such is the effect of being in the presence of a wise father. Just when I thought I couldn't possibly meet another wonderful father, God said, "Yes, you can." Don was available. He answered God's call. He always does.

5

NATURAL

"I believe the world is too plastic and consumeristic...
childhood is lost in the process."

✠

Paul Grenier, D.C.

PALEO DAD

Cain Credicott
Oregon

J.J. – While I was writing this book, a couple of people I knew in the medical field told me they ate Paleo. Both of them radiated health and energy. Eager to learn more, I read about it online and in Paleo Magazine and found that it's a way of eating and living adopted from our Paleolithic ancestors, which honors our bodies' genetic design.

I then decided to include a father who lives this healthy lifestyle in this book. I emailed Cain Credicott, the Founder and Editor in Chief of Paleo Magazine, to see if he'd be open to being interviewed. I received an enthusiastic reply within five minutes. He said he didn't know if he had much wisdom to share, but he'd be happy to be interviewed. I laughed to myself, for several fathers I interviewed questioned if they had any wisdom to offer, yet after speaking with them, I found they were filled with wisdom about fatherhood, living and loving.
Cain was no exception.

—

In 2008 when I was diagnosed with celiac disease and food allergies, I decided to eat vegan and a gluten-free diet. However, I didn't seem to feel much better. I had heard about a diet known as the Paleo diet, an ancient way of eating that excludes grains and refined sugar. The diet focuses on real, whole foods, such as lean meats, fresh fruits and vegetables. After one month, I felt so much better that I started *Paleo Magazine* to help more people transform their diet and lives for the better. I also implemented the diet at home with my daughters to give them the best nutrition possible.

As a Paleo Dad, I explained to my girls why it's important to eat healthy foods and what happens when they eat harmful ones, to listen to what their body is hungry for, and how it reacts to certain foods. My family has eaten Paleo for several years now, but we each do our own version of it. It works because we've learned which foods give us energy and help us feel our best.

Living Paleo isn't just a matter of food though; it's a lifestyle. Paleo wisdom suggests that there are some benefits of life pre-Internet, pre-electronics and pre-agriculture. But it's not about reverting to the caveman days.

The Paleo lifestyle advocates checking out of modern life on occasion where we turn off the iPad, Facebook, etc. and spend time in nature. As a family, my wife and daughters and I, get outside regularly and enjoy the sun. We ski, swim, paddle board, play tennis and take our Labrador Retriever on walks and hikes. Our lifestyle is also about connecting with others face-to-face. We spend at least one to two meals a day together and hang out by a fire at night. We chat about our day and listen to one another's random thoughts. It's our last chance to connect with our 'tribe', and then we go to bed.

Prior to gas and electricity, man had only fire for lighting and did not stay up all hours of the night with artificial light. When my family watches TV at night, we wear amber glasses to protect our eyes from the glare and blue light. This light suppresses melatonin and prevents a good night's sleep. We have low blue lights in our home and on my daughters' nightstands. The girls wear amber glasses when they read in bed at night, and I have an amber screen on my iPad. We also go to bed early to get sufficient sleep and honor nature's cycle of light and dark.

Paleo living is about thriving, so it's important that my daughters feel empowered and value themselves. I teach them to take responsibility for their behavior so that they'll make choices which bring them the results they want. If they come home from school and are upset that someone wasn't nice to them, I tell them that it doesn't matter what the other person thinks of them. I also model this for my daughters. I'll try a new idea no matter what someone else thinks, and if it doesn't work, I'll try another strategy. When I started *Paleo Magazine* two and a half years ago, I had no idea how to do it since I'd never written or published a magazine. I didn't let that stop me though, because I was determined to share the valuable information about the Paleo life with the public. My kids saw my errors and how much work and stress was involved. I didn't hide that from them because I wanted them to see that I'm not perfect and that mistakes happen when your learning something new, and that's okay. This is especially hard for my youngest daughter. Recently, she took a grade level exam which tested her knowledge on things she knew and things she didn't. She was not supposed to know everything, but she cried when she saw her mistakes. I told her that mistakes are a natural part of learning, but if she tried her best, she's a success regardless of her score.

My father taught me not to take myself too seriously. I pass this teaching onto my daughters to help them de-stress and have a lighter approach to life. It's challenging to be the one guy living with three women. Even if I don't relate to my daughter's issues, I'm always there to comfort and talk with them. I'll sit with them and rub their back. I always offer them strong fatherly support to help them work through their problems.

My oldest daughter has ADD, and verbal communication can be challenging for her. She thinks something in her mind but it doesn't always come out clearly, and I misinterpret her words, get impatient and discipline her. After I think it over, I realize that she probably meant something else. We'll talk it over to clear things up and I'll apologize for my hasty judgement. More than once I've gone into my daughters' room at night and woken them up to apologize and make peace. I want to make sure that everything is okay before we go to sleep.

I hope that my parenting efforts lead my daughters to be happy adults, doing what they want in life. My father worked at the same company for years and had dreams he never acted upon, such as opening a bookstore, and he died with 'what-ifs'. I never want to have any 'what-if's' and I don't want my my daughters to either. As an entrepreneur, I'm the opposite of my father. My daughters are also budding entrepreneurs. My oldest is writing a children's book, and after the text is done, we'll find an illustrator for it and then publish it. My youngest makes T-shirt designs. She creates the design, and we load it onto a website which we got for her. People can then buy her design and T-shirt through the online store.

I love watching my daughters grow up and turn into people with their own pursuits and opinions. They are little people blossoming. It's fun seeing them be independent. They are my fountain of youth; they keep me young and grounded. I love my daughters, and being their father is awesome. I wouldn't change it for anything!

J.J. – After talking to Cain and learning more about the power of living Paleo to help us heal and thrive, I went Paleo! I feel healthier, more alive and energized. I'm now a modern-day woman with a Paleolithic palate.

Today, let's live Paleo: eat and enjoy real food; connect with people rather than electronics; breathe deeply, then smile to de-stress; and go to bed early for a full night's sleep.

SAFE AND SERENE– LIVING IN THE GERMAN COUNTRYSIDE

Georg Schneider, Ph.D.
Germany

I had a happy childhood growing up in the German countryside. My father taught school while my mother took care of us children. I became a teacher as well, a Professor of Computer Science at the University of Applied Sciences in Trier.

My father always respected me enough to take me seriously. We often discussed life's issues. I admired the way he lived and raised me so much, that I wanted to provide the same quality upbringing for my two children. I talk to my kids. I don't just bark commands, but I explain the reason for things. If it's cold outside, I might say, "Wear a jacket instead of just a T-shirt. I don't want you to get sick."

As a father, I enjoy being with my family the most. I love to come home after work and spend time with my children. I read to them, and we go on bike rides. We make pancakes, and I let my daughter help by measuring the flour. I want her to be confident that she can do things on her own. I want my children to have endurance and try new things. I see my little girl's frustration when she struggles trying to dress a doll or build something with Legos. She wants to give up. I tell her, "Don't give up; you can do it. Try again." My wife is French, and we speak both German and French in our home. At times my daughter mixes the two languages together. I am patient and tell her to think and speak again in order to learn each language correctly. I also speak English, and my daughter and I watch videos like *Barney* to help her learn English.

After living in the United States and doing research at Princeton, I decided to move back to the countryside where I grew up. My children deserve to play outside alone like I did, and the countryside is safe; they can play with friends and walk to school on their own. I want them to explore the nearby town, to become responsible and independent.

Raising children is so rewarding, but it's not easy. It's a twenty-four hour a day job. Supporting my family without financial struggles and concerns usually keeps me free from worry and in a good mood. If I'm in a bad mood though, I work to keep myself under control. And thanks to the joy of
living in the tranquil countryside with my family, I'm never in a bad mood for long.

Today, let's bring the serenity of the German countryside into our lives and live at peace with the people, tasks and situations we face.

YOGA DAD

Gabriel Hall
California

My father gave me the freedom to make my own way in the world and not just be a small version of himself. His name was Robert Leslie Hall, Jr., and he purposely named me Gabriel, (not junior) to set a foundation for me to develop my unique identity. My father courageously broke away from the 1950s model of fatherhood, where the man focused on his work and was a stoic, behind-the-scenes father.

He went to Cal Berkeley in the 1960's amidst the tumult of the Vietnam War and embraced the free-living, hippie spirit. He chose a less financially lucrative career than his father, to spend more time with his children so that when he was home, he was fully present with us, instead of being preoccupied with a stressful, demanding job.

My parents did not give me specific religious dogmas to follow, and Shiva and Buddha statues in our home fostered my curiosity about spirituality. I explored conventional wisdom and Eastern philosophy such as yoga, mysticism, Daoism and Hinduism.

I formally began studying yoga when I was nineteen, but I had long since practiced it informally since the age five when I was determined to stand on my head in perfect control and stillness! I later became a yoga teacher and have now taught for twenty-four years. I opened Yoga World Studios in 1997 as the first and now longest-running yoga studio in Long Beach, CA.

When I became the father of Alice, now age six, the yoga philosophy and practice became an intrinsic part of my fathering. As both a father and person, I live and pass on the wisdom of the eight limbs of the Yoga Sutras. These limbs serve as guidelines to live a meaningful and purposeful life.

One Yoga Sutra involves developing one's physicality and spirituality through practicing yoga postures. Alice does yoga and learns the discipline from my wife and myself, and from a private teacher. She gains movement education by learning proper techniques for running, jumping and squatting. Yoga has also been physical therapy for her and has loosened some of her tight muscles. Children are natural yogis for they're more flexible than most adults. I also recommend yoga for parents to relieve stress and gain tools for total life wellness.

Another Yoga Sutra involves gaining breath control to attain greater self-discipline. Our breath has psychological effects on our nervous system. People can change their psyche, feelings and actions just by changing how they breathe. If people are fearful and breathing quickly, they can slow down their breath to attain more peace. Through my yoga tutelage of Alice, she learns to control her breath to help her relax if she's scared.

I also practice and teach mindful meditation, which is where distracting thoughts and feelings are observed non- judgmentally in order to detach from them and gain insight. This helps me to focus my attention and calm my mind and body. I also teach mindful meditation to my daughter to help her be more intentional about her behavior. She learns to be aware of her feelings, but not overwhelmed by them. If Alice feels angry, she can be aware of what she's feeling, but choose a peaceful path instead of lashing out. An acronym for mindful meditation is COAL. "C" is for curiosity, "O" for openness, "A" for acceptance and "L" for loving kindness. Alice is a teaching assistant in one of my classes and gives notes of loving kindness, such as, "You're awesome," to students.

The yoga principle of the "discipline of freedom" guides many of my parenting choices. Kids need structure and boundaries to learn to be responsible, respect others and relate well with others. My wife and I give Alice specific boundaries and the freedom to choose within them. For instance, we may give her four vegetable choices so that her boundary is for nutritious food. Then we let her choose which one she'd like, knowing that any one she chooses will serve her well. This helps her learn healthy boundaries and make positive choices within them.

Through my years of yoga and self-reflection from my practice, I'm highly aware of my thoughts, feelings and behaviors. I'm conscious of what I model for Alice, for I know she will learn by observing what I do. Although I'm careful about my actions, I still live authentically and don't pretend to be a perfect parent. When I've been a less than ideal model, I discuss it with Alice. If we're driving and I may make an impatient remark about a driver, I tell Alice that my comment wasn't the best and that a kinder, more patient response would've been better. She learns that she doesn't have to be perfect and can improve her behavior as she becomes wiser.

Fatherhood might not be for everybody, but it's definitely for me. I've treasured all of Alice's years, and as long as she's engaged and enjoying what she's doing, I'm happy. We read books together, like favorites by Dr. Seuss and Mo Williams. Our reading connection started when Alice was in the womb, and my wife and I read to her every day. I loved coddling her as a baby when she was wrapped up in her swaddle and putting her to sleep.

Now that she's older, we do art, wrestle and play theater games. One of our favorites is when Alice pretends to be a little lost girl in the forest, our dog is the wolf, and I play the bear, who rescues the girl from the wolf. Sometimes Alice and I let loose and laugh from being "muy loco"–kind of crazy.

Alice surprises us with sweet acts of love. She'll disappear into her bedroom and come out with a card telling us how much she loves us. It's incredible to see my heart in someone else's body. As Alice grows, I hope that she lives well, loves fully and deeply enjoys her time on the planet.

Fatherhood is unbelievably rich, deep, complex, moving–the most important job I've ever had. One of my greatest joys is being Alice's father. Although fatherhood is challenging and all encompassing, I never regret becoming a father. I love the responsibility of it. I am indebted to my father who was a good role model. Because of him I knew what I wanted to be when I grew up–a father myself! I love watching Alice grow up in front of me, steering her in a positive direction, inspiring her and being inspired by her. I see life again through eyes that are young as she learns things for the first time. As I watch her discover the world, I discover it again. Fatherhood is amazing. I love it. I deeply love it.

Today, let's practice some yoga moments and take C.O.A.L.- adding a little Curiosity, Openness, Acceptance and Loving kindness into our lives.

NATURAL LIVING

Paul Grenier, D.C.
Wisconsin

    I grew up on a farm in North Dakota with four brothers and two sisters. We lived thirteen miles outside of a town that consisted of a whopping 850 people. We raised 200 head of cattle and harvested fields of grain such as barley, wheat and sunflower. I now live with my own family in a rural area in Wisconsin just four miles outside of a town of 4,000 people (just a bit bigger than when I was a kid).

    Our home is on a six-acre lot with two barns. My children bike to school, and we spend peaceful evenings together at home. We don't watch much TV but make our own fun, going outside for walks and cross-country skiing. My kids love to run, dig in the dirt, climb trees, play in the barns and spend time with their animals. My family lives more like it was in the past, without much technology. There are snowmen to make during the winter, and grass to roll around in during the summer. They use boxes, sheets and blankets to make indoor forts; and leaves, branches, tin, old tires and items they've dug out of the barn to make outdoor forts.

    I want my children to be free spirits who are close to God and nature and connected to the vibrational force of the earth. This was my own father's greatest gift to me: He stood back and allowed us to make our own choices and take our own path. He never judged us and would give his input only when asked. I'd often discuss matters with my father at turning points in high school and college. He listened for an hour or however long was needed. I always felt that my father loved me and was proud of me even if I made mistakes.

I have three children of my own, and I pray to be more like my father. I don't want to be overprotective of them. I let my kids climb trees and get a bruise or two, but I would never let any real harm come to them. There is a balance to this thing called, "Fatherhood." I want to keep that balance in every area. I work three days a week as a chiropractor, and we live frugally in a small, but comfortable house in an affordable area. We shop at Goodwill. We'd rather spend our money on traveling and visiting family members. One time, I took the year off work, and we traveled throughout the United States in an RV. We enjoyed a lot of play, closeness and laughter. My children entertained themselves and laughed freely without inhibitions. When I saw them express such pure joy, I knew I was doing right as a parent.

I never went to a doctor growing up, and my children have also never been to a medical doctor. They had home births and have received chiropractic adjustments since birth. I trust in my children's bodies to heal themselves. They've had fevers and vomited, and their bodies have taken care of everything they've had thus far.

We are an environment friendly family, we reduce, reuse and recycle. At Christmas, my kids get few toys, and they're homemade and recycled. For one of my daughter's birthdays, we asked guests to only bring handmade or previously-used gifts. My children have played with used Legos and dinosaurs. My wife and I used cloth diapers instead of plastic because of the dangers of the toxic chemicals within them and to reduce waste from disposing them in landfills. We don't use soap on our children, and their skin doesn't peel and is extremely soft, maintaining its natural oils. People comment on how our children's skin glows. My oldest daughter washes her hair infrequently to maintain its natural oils. My family also uses shade instead of sunscreen.

In today's world, children are hindered from being and living their best and one reason is due to a poor diet. My wife breast-fed our children to give them the best nutrition, for the mother's milk is bio-specific for each child, and bottles can't duplicate that. After being breast-fed, my children have had green algae smoothies every day. They eat live organic foods and very little sugar. They have never had soda pop but drink juice instead.

My children attend a school which honors their natural development. They engage in free play, games and music to stimulate their creativity and connect their brain to their heart. Their teachers tell them many stories and have them do activities, such as dancing the movement of what they hear in stories, to use their whole body in the learning process.

My wife and I read chapter books without pictures to our children so that they listen, create their own pictures in their minds and later draw their own illustrations. One of our favorites are the Laura Ingalls Wilder books. I believe that the world is too plastic and consumeristic and that children's childhoods are lost in this process.

My goal is for my children to express their God- given potential. I hope they'll be independent, empowered, connected to family, and loving to others. I also hope they'll graduate from high school happy, at peace and equipped to create their own destiny. I want them to feel complete with their own power source through God. We are born with the opportunity to be self-sufficient and have the universal power with us. Many have lost their trust in this, and I hope that my children never will.

I believe children need their mother full time the first two years of their life. I support my wife financially so she doesn't have to work and can be home with our children. I make sure she takes breaks and has time with her friends to maintain her well-being. I also help with getting the children up every morning and putting them to bed each evening.

My greatest experience with my children was the birth of my youngest daughter. We have a birthing room in our home, and my daughter had a water birth. My wife's labor began at 9:00 a.m. and my daughter was born at 10:15 p.m. At the time my eldest daughter was six and my son was three. During the birth process, my kids knew that something special was occurring. My daughter gave her mother a massage and said, "You can do this, Mom." She saw the baby's head crowning and got in the tub with her mother. It was a magical, spiritual process. A special connection was formed between them all from this, and it continues to grow.

I want to keep this magical connection with my family, especially as they grow up and live lives of their own. My desire is for them to continue to live that natural, relaxed lifestyle no matter where life takes them and to pass it on to their own children someday.

Today, let's live naturally, love completely and make a few more snowmen and blanket forts with our children.

6

HUMBLE

*"Every dad makes mistakes;
I can't feel too badly about them for there is
no such thing as a perfect dad."*

✢

Brian Hurnard

GO FOR BROKE

Jim Makino
California

J.J. – I interviewed Jim Makino at the Japanese American National Museum in Los Angeles, CA.

—

Many people living at that time heard the news of the bombing of Pearl Harbor by the Japanese in 1941 on the radio. My parents had come from Japan and first settled in Hawaii before moving to California. They owned several markets, and I helped out the family business by delivering bread, butter and other items to customers.

Our peaceful routine life ended when the U.S. government issued orders which forced Japanese-Americans living on the West Coast to be put in War Relocation Centers. My family and I were taken by train to Santa Fe, New Mexico. I was confused; I had no idea where we were going. Soldiers held guns on us because we were classified as "4C" (enemy aliens). I was a twenty-year-old United States citizen and certainly not an alien. My father told my family, "Don't worry, we'll manage."

Shortly after this, in 1943, I filled out the War Relocation Authority Questionnaire. It was designed to determine the loyalty of inmates to be released as "resettlers" and volunteers to the planned 442nd Regimental Combat Team composed of all-Nisei (second-generation Americans born of Japanese parents). The survey was given to all men and women seventeen years and older. Questions 27 and 28 were known as the "loyalty" questions. Question 27 asked, "Are you willing to serve in the Armed Forces of the United States on combat duty wherever ordered?" Question 28 asked, "Will you swear unqualified allegiance to the United States of America and faithfully defend the United States from any or all attack by foreign or domestic forces, and forswear any form of allegiance or obedience to the Japanese Emperor, or any other foreign government, power or organization?" A "Yes" answer to both questions meant renunciation of Japanese citizenship, and a "No" to either question branded the person as disloyal and a troublemaker.[2] I answered, "Yes" to both questions and joined the 442nd.

After a training period, I went to fight in Europe. The 442nd became the most heavily decorated unit with the highest casualty rate for its size and length of service in the history of the U.S. Army. Many of the soldiers were from Hawaii, and our unit motto was, "Go for Broke," from the Hawaiian pidgin phrase used by crap shooters who risked all their money in one roll of the dice. Our mindset was to risk greatly to show our loyalty to the U.S. and to help end the war so that our families could get out of the internment camps.

In one of our campaigns, we broke through the Gothic Line in northern Italy. The Germans built the Gothic Line along the top of the steep Apennine Mountains. Fifteen thousand Italian slave laborers drilled into the solid rock to make gun trenches and 2,376 machine gun nests, which they reinforced with concrete. The Allies had unsuccessfully attempted to destroy these positions for five months. At the beginning of April 1945, our unit was called in and destroyed the positions within four days. We climbed up the back of the 3,000-foot-high mountain and were told to be quiet. Two soldiers fell and

[2] http://caamedia.org/jainternment/camps/questions.html

did not make a sound. We broke through the line, and hundreds of Germans surrendered. Less than two weeks later, on May 7, 1945, Germany surrendered.

I was twenty-three years old after the war and eventually married and became a father. My wife and I had decided to adopt a child and were able to bring home a beautiful baby girl. I remember the day the social worker called to tell us the baby was ours. I was overcome with joy at becoming a father. I also felt overwhelmed about the responsibility of parenting this fragile little girl who was solely dependent on my wife and me. My joy overrode my concern though, and I felt blessed to welcome my baby girl into our home. When my daughter later learned that she had been adopted, she, too, felt blessed knowing that she had been specially chosen by her parents. I am now a proud grandfather and continue to "Go for Broke" with my love and support towards my family. My hope is that none of my precious loved ones ever have to go through the hell of war that I did, and I work to educate others of this reality.

J.J. – When I interviewed Jim, he had the "Go for Broke" motto on his belt buckle, tie clip and book bag, with an emblem of the Statue of Liberty holding the torch of freedom. Jim also showed me the medals he received in the war, and after I exclaimed, "Wow," he replied, "No big deal." He is a humble, yet mighty hero.

Today, as a tribute to the 442nd, let's "Go for Broke" and take a risk for at least one of our goals and say a prayer of blessing for all those who fought in the 442nd and their families.

REFLECTIONS ON FATHERHOOD - A LIFETIME COMMITMENT

Brian Hurnard
Australia

J.J. – I met Brian through his daughter, Elizabeth, who has been a pen pal of mine for over thirty years. Once on a trip to the U.S., Elizabeth and her entire family visited us, and we all had such a wonderful time. They have such an amazing Aussie sense of humor, I knew years later, as I searched for wise fathers, that Brian would be a valuable addition from the "Land Down Under."

—

Raising a family and being a dad is an endless journey of highs and lows, good times and bad; accidents and sickness, holidays, school days, driving lessons and everything in between. One thing is sure, problems that loomed so big and dramatic at the time, fade into perspective as the years go by. At the end of the day, it's all worthwhile when your kids give you a big hug and say that you are the best dad in the world.

My own father, although a good man with so many great qualities, gave me the most profound lessons in life from his mistakes. My father struggled with prejudice. When I was in my twenties, I made a conscious decision to learn from his attitudes and avoid his downfalls. This was helped immeasurably by my close relationship with my father-in- law, who embodied all my father's good points, but added in compassion, generosity and understanding. I'd like my children to follow the same philosophy and sort out the traits which they wish to perpetuate.

Our kids are all grown up now and in their late forties. We have five wonderful grandchildren and cherish their friendships. Our two daughters lived overseas for many years and recently have returned to their home town. It is one of my greatest joys to see them often and spend quality time with them. They all own their own homes and our son does, too. I delight in helping them with work, gardening, maintenance and redecoration. I guess this role fits me well.

There is no practical training course for the occupation of father. It feels at times we are winging it from day one! Every dad makes mistakes; I can't feel too badly about them for there is no such thing as a perfect dad. I learned from my own parents and childhood and used what was good, hopefully not repeating their mistakes. We can all learn from the bad, and although this job of father is a huge responsibility, I leave room for plenty of love and fun.

Today, let's emulate something positive we learned from our father or father figure.

HELPFUL AND KIND

Jon Meyer
California

J.J. – When I called Jon Meyer to ask if I could interview him for this book, his first question was, "How can I help you?" As he was leaving at the end of the interview, he asserted that he would help in any way he could.

People's character shines through in their words and actions, and Jon's life as a father and educator demonstrates his helpfulness to others. He blends this helpful spirit with kindness so that the receiver feels encouraged and refreshed by his genuineness. The Talmud says, "The highest form of wisdom is kindness." Jon Meyer exemplifies this wisdom.

—

I gained a strong foundation of love growing up from the emphasis my father placed on family. We had large family get-togethers, many in which my father's brothers played the piano and sang barbershop quartet. My older brother and I would join in the singing. We had an RCA Victrola and made records with a megaphone, which we played on a turntable. How I looked forward to those times! Since it's October, we're planning our next large gathering for Thanksgiving. The beat carries on.

I also learned kindness by my father's example. He was a high school teacher, and football and baseball coach. One of his baseball player's fathers said that his only "fault" was that there was "too much of Jesus Christ in him." The teenage boys were eager to play for him because of his great ability to train and inspire them to success, all based on his foundation of kindness. Many of his baseball team members later played professionally, and two were in the World Series.

As a father, I desired to model positive attributes and actions, like my father did, to my own children, and assist them wherever I could. Our kids are older now, but my wife and I speak to them often on the phone and offer support, guidance, and a safe place to share what they are going through. I wonder about the future my children and grandchildren will face. I take each day as it comes and keep my heart open for whatever the need may be. As Omar Khayyam wisely wrote in the *Rubayyat*, "...make the most of what we may yet spend, before we too into the dust descend."

I hope that my children and grandchildren will live a life as joyous and fulfilling as the one that my wife and I have had the privilege to lead.

As my children were growing up, I worked as a high school teacher and elementary and high school principal. The importance of education was modeled in our home. We had a designated time at night when the television, radio, and phone were turned off, and my children studied for school. My wife and I discussed curfew times with our kids to determine a sensible time to be home each night. It was also a non- negotiable–we all have dinner together. If one of my kids had an upcoming activity that conflicted with a family dinner, we rearranged our schedule in order to share the meal together. It's critical for families to have a point where they meet in the day as a unit to nurture and solidify their relationships. I am so proud that both my children have earned their master's degrees and are highly successful in their professions. My son is a high school teacher and football coach, and my daughter is a physical therapist.

After I retired, I ran for the Long Beach School Board and was honored to win the position in my district. My goal on the Board is to serve the best interests of the students, and I enjoy making decisions for that purpose. I believe that the main issue facing public education today is working to overcome the poverty and dysfunction in homes and the disparity that results with children who don't grow up with the same educational advantages as those in more affluent homes. As an educator and father, giving our young people every opportunity to succeed is near and dear to my heart.

I am thankful for my professional success and the opportunity to serve on the School Board. I've learned, though, not to get bitten by the bug of success. It takes a strong person to not be carried away by its lure. It's crucial to continue to build and foster relationships with family and friends, to laugh, and enjoy a balanced life.

A motto I'd like to pass onto my kids and others comes from Aldous Huxley, the English writer and humanist. When John F. Kennedy asked Huxley what advice he had for others before he passed away, he replied, "Try to be a little kinder."

Today, let's be helpful and kind in every possible occasion.

INTEGRITY

Bob Gilder
Oregon

J.J. – The evening that Bob and I planned to talk, he called to ask if we could speak later that night; he'd had a full day on the golf course and wanted to have dinner with his wife. Bob is a professional golfer, whose many accomplishments include winning six tournaments on the PGA Tour, ten on the Champions Tour, and tying sixth in the 1992 U.S. Open. My vision of a professional golfer, having only seen them on beautiful courses throughout the world on television, was a life of glamour focused on golf.

Later that night, I learned that although he is one of the world's finest golfers, he is a family man first. After his work was done on the golf course, he was a committed husband and father. As he spoke of wife and kids, his voice was filled with energy and good cheer, which I imagined were due to living the fruits of life–having a career which he loves and a family which he cherishes even more.

—

About eighty-five miles south of Portland, Oregon, is Corvallis, the town where I grew up. My father built custom and spec homes there, and he taught me his trade as I worked alongside of him. He was an easy-going man who let me do my own thing. Growing up, I played all kinds of sports, built homes with my father during school vacations, and golfed in between. My father fully supported all my athletic pursuits.

When I was I in the ninth grade, I met the woman I would eventually marry. We have been together since we were fourteen years old and have a wonderful marriage to this day. We also still live in Corvallis along with our two adult sons, daughter, and nine grandchildren. Since my father passed away a year ago, my ninety-one-year-old mother moved in with us. I'm blessed that my whole family lives so close and that we are all welcome in each other's homes.

After college, my pursuit of golf became more serious, and I started touring. In 1975, I qualified for the PGA Tour. I golfed on that tour twnety-five years for thirty-two to thirty- four weeks per year. I am now in my fifteenth year on the Champions Tour, and I travel about twnety-eight weeks a year. During my early touring years, my wife and I took our kids with us, but when they grew old enough to start school, my wife stayed home. I tried never to be away from home more than two weeks at a time. I called my family nearly every night. It was challenging to be away so much during my kids' growing up years, but to make up for it, I spent close, quality time with them when I was home. I enjoyed just being with them and doing sports. Because I needed to protect myself physically, I could not engage in any reckless sports. Since golf is my livelihood, an injury could severely curb the family income, I could not risk having a broken bone and miss touring. If my family went skiing, I drove the car and watched. I love golf, but my focus was on taking care of my family and providing for them. This meant being a spectator, at times, in some of the fun.

Fatherhood is more than just words. I've sought to be an example to my kids. My mother once told me, "You're no better than anyone else, and you're no worse. Don't treat people above or below you. We're all equal." I instilled this philosophy into my kids to help them respect and value themselves and others equally.

I also model being a man of integrity for my kids and teach them to be honest whether they're alone or someone is watching. The profession of golf calls for a high level of integrity amongst the players. In golf, we call penalties on ourselves, unlike football or basketball, here there is no referee. Golf is an independent game; often, we're the only ones who see what we do. Golfers could get away with anything, but we choose not to. I have both experienced and seen other pros lose thousands of dollars and tournaments by taking the higher road of integrity.

My kids have learned by watching me play by the rules in golf and life. Once when we were in a hotel, one of my kids said that he could take the towel out of the room. I asked him how he'd feel if he owned the hotel and every guest took the towels, and then he had to go buy new towels to replace the stolen ones. I said, "The towel is the hotel's, not ours. We don't steal." Whether in little things or in big things, I wanted my son to realize that living honestly was the best way to live.

My sons have often caddied for me when I have been on tour. One of my favorite memories was when my oldest son caddied for me at the Masters when he was sixteen years old. It was great fun to have them both on the course with me, and we always grew closer from the experience. My kids saw what I went through as a professional, and they learned from the tough decisions that I made during games. We traveled yearly to Disney World where I played in a tournament there for about seventeen years. I golfed five to six hours during the day and then joined them at night in the park. It was exhausting, but spending time with my family always renewed me, and seeing the joy on my kids' faces and sharing their fun and happiness in the magic kingdom made it all worthwhile.

At sixty-five, I continue to spend hours practicing golf. Excellence only comes from hard work and a commitment to give life your all. In golf, there's always someone better, ready to knock you down. I get back up every time though, and I've instilled this same resiliency in my kids. I've taught them to accept failure as a part of the path to greater wisdom and success. About 150 guys compete in professional tournaments, and only one can win. In twenty-five years on the PGA Tour, I played over 1,000 tournaments and won six. But it's that challenge that makes me give my 110%. Recently my oldest son applied for a job for which he didn't have the exact training. He didn't know if he should go for it. It was an intimidating situation, but he was courageous and undertook the challenge. He got the position and is now enjoying great success in it. I'm so proud of him for taking the risk.

I've tried to be an example to my kids of never giving up and always persevering to excel. What keeps me going? My competitiveness and drive to win. I persist because I love the ongoing learning, challenges, and striving to get better. You can bowl a perfect game, but you can't golf a perfect game. I visualize making a really great shot and imagine what it would feel like in my body. Then, when I hit that perfect shot, I feel exhilarated. It's the best feeling. It keeps me coming back year after year to the green.

As I look to my future, I know that I'll continue to take on the challenges that lay ahead of me in golf. Most importantly though, I'll never quit being a father who loves his kids. On and off the course, I'm a dad, and I love it!

INTEGRITY

Today, let's conduct ourselves with integrity and persevere with any challenges life presents. Wisdom and success are sure to come.

A LIFE OF GIVING BACK

Hunt Harris
Illinois

J.J. – I read about Hunt Harris in the Spring 2002 Phi Beta Kappa publication, The Key Reporter.[3] I was so impressed by his commitment to serving his community and his honesty in sharing about his life, that I knew I'd found another wise father. His staggering generosity impressed me. He gave almost $400,000 for the purchase of new computers to his local school system, which helped raise students' standardized test scores. I knew I wanted to interview this genuinely generous man. The Phi Beta Kappa Office in Washington D.C. helped me contact him for the book, and I share his story here to pass on his wisdom and inspiration.

—

My greatest challenge as a father was dealing with the two-year period of seeing my youngest son's attempt to overcome a prescription drug addiction and then passing away from an overdose. My wife and I thought we were doing the right thing as parents, and yet this tragedy occurred. How do you cope with such a loss? We cried a lot and found some solace and relief in knowing that our son is now at peace.

I would tell other parents going through this to acknowledge the problem your child has; don't be in denial. Treatment centers are not thirty-day cures, and recovery is a lifelong pro-

---

[3]Phi Beta Kappa The Key Reporter, Spring 2002, Vol. 67, Num. 3, P. 7-8

cess. No matter how much you love your child, it is his or her addiction and not yours.

I experienced my own life-threatening ordeal when I was diagnosed with cancer of the tongue, tonsils, and lymph nodes of the neck. I immediately stopped my work trading stocks and commodities and focused on my treatments. I was overwhelmed by the outpouring of prayers and encouragement during my recovery.

Traumatic events can stimulate personal growth though, and from this experience, I gained greater empathy for those going through cancer or any disease. I learned a new appreciation for the indiscriminate nature of the disease. I saw some people that I went through treatment with die, and others recover. Recovering and overcoming such adversity made me a better person and my family stronger. I learned to accept what I could not change and to fight for what I could. I became more relaxed, flexible, and less driven. Trading with high stakes was extremely stressful, and I stopped putting myself in such stressful situations. I got a business partner to share the work and lower the stress.

I prioritize spending time with my family and giving attention to them and my community. My father taught me the importance of giving back to the community. He served on the local school board, and we always had foster kids in our home. Thanks to early success in business, I started a second career at age thirty-nine in philanthropy. My wife and I established a family foundation and have raised funds for the United Way. I also helped create a unified hospital system in the Illinois Quad Cities. When the two hospital systems in the area merged, the community saved tens of millions of dollars in capital costs, and the hospitals saved tens of millions of dollars in operating expenses. The hospitals' quality also improved. I want my kids to have this same philanthropist heart, giving in whatever way possible, to help others.

It's all about pursuing a balanced life for me. I pray and meditate daily and express thanks for the blessings I've been given. I pray for my family and business relations, our leaders, those who are sick and suffering, peace in troubled areas, and guidance on how I can give back to my community. I also focus on living a healthy life and being physically fit.

I am grateful to have raised a son, daughter and granddaughter. I helped them develop their talents and taught them to have integrity and to give back to their community. Though we have gone through tragedies, we have grown through them and now give back what we have learned to others.

***Today, let's live in balance
and give back to our community.***

7

INVESTING

"Although I lead a financial institute where people invest money, my greatest investment has been the time, care, support and guidance I've given my kids. I've reaped priceless dividends from this investment."

✥

Jeff Napper

A FATHER'S IMPACT

Chris Steinhauser
California

J.J. – I interviewed Chris at his office at the Long Beach Unified School District (LBUSD), where he serves as Superintendent of Schools for the third largest school district in California. During the middle of our talk, he got a phone call for work. I figured our time was over and expected to leave. Chris then said he would return the call after our meeting. I was stunned, for he chose instead to speak with me over an hour about fatherhood. Once again, I'd met another wise father, lovingly devoted to his kids.

—

My father was a high school drop-out. When he was in his twenties, he saw the value in finishing his education and enrolled in adult school and received his high school diploma. He became a baker, and through hard work and the educational certificates he earned, he rose to the top and became the superintendent of the baking company, where he worked. "Education is the key to everything," my father said, "because it opens many doors." After I graduated from high school, my father let me live in our house, rent free, as long as I pursued my schoolwork. It was my father's way of stressing the importance of education.

Once, I remember visiting the bakery my father supervised, along with my brothers, to watch my father at work. He said that there's nothing wrong with this type of work, but he wanted my brothers and me to be educated and have options. Working as a baker was arduous, tedious, and dangerous at times. Breads and other items came out of the oven at 400° temperatures, and although the bakers wore large gloves, they still received severe burns.

With six boys to provide for, our family often struggled financially. My father worked long hours to provide for us. He was a wise financial manager though, and he taught me a balanced financial formula for living. My father said that ideally 70% of one's income would be for living expenses, 10% for charity, 10% for emergencies, and 10% for recreation and vacations. He told me to pay my bills before anything else and to have six months of mortgage payments in the bank. He also taught me to be independent and said that if I wanted a car, I needed to work, save my money, and then purchase it. I followed my father's guidance and bought my own car.

When I became a father, I passed this financial wisdom down to my son, now twenty-seven, and my daughter, age twenty-five. When my kids got jobs at sixteen, I insisted that they save 50% of their paychecks. Overtime, each of my kids bought their own cars just as I'd done. My kids are now considering buying homes, which is a large accomplishment for young adults, especially in the expensive Southern California housing market.

Being a father is the greatest thing in the world. What a blessing to have experienced the joys in each stage of my children's lives! When they were young, we planted flowers in the backyard, read *Good Night Moon* and *Runaway Bunny*, and played games. I was my daughter's beauty shop stand-in. You should have seen all the clips she put in my hair! It was tough to see them grow up and navigate those teenage years. All those hormonal changes and becoming independent, longing to drive-I handled this time by having open communication with them. If they were going out, I wanted them to share where they were going and let me know if they'd be late. My parents had been strict, which had been effective for me. My wife and I were also strict and had high expectations for our kids. They were expected to go to college, and then it was their choice about what to do in life. My son is now a teacher, and my daughter is an event planner.

Parenting is a team effort. My parents were 100% partners in raising my brothers and me. They never disagreed in front of us and presented a united front. If they had a disagreement, they discussed it privately. If my brothers or I were rewarded or punished, both parents were involved. My wife and I follow the same teamwork approach. Due to my busy professional life as a teacher, administrator, and now Superintendent of Schools of the Long Beach Unified School District (LBUSD), I have little flexibility in my schedule. My wife coached my kids' athletic teams since I was not able to with my work, yet I still attended their sporting events.

Now that my kids are in their twenties, we enjoy our times together more than ever. We are best friends and go to movies, music programs, and athletic events such as college football games. Two to three times a week, I go walking with my son. We still take vacations together. One of my favorites was when we all went to Paris one Christmas and attended Mass at Notre Dame. I believe the key to our successful relationships is the respect we have for one another.

Parenting is all about modeling, and the only handbook for being a father is one's own parents. My father taught me it was important to follow through on my word. One time, my father said that if I got all A's on my report card, I would receive a new five-speed Schwinn bike. When I earned all A's, I knew that the bike would be a difficult expense for my father since we had limited resources. I told him I didn't need it. My father replied that he'd follow through on his promise, and I got that bike. I respected my father for that; I knew I could trust him always. I have cultivated this kind of relationship with my children.

My parents hoped that my brothers and I would live better lives than they did. I have attained this, and I hope that my children live better lives than I have. I am proud of my kids. My daughter helps those with special needs and recently volunteered at the Ronald McDonald House. My son is in the Music Ministry at his church. During the summer, he serves as the Director of Aquatic Camps at Alamitos Bay, where he helps kids with water sports and provides extra counseling for those in need.

My original dream was to be a high school history teacher and coach. Instead, I became an elementary school teacher, principal, and now Superintendent for LBUSD. As I rose in administration though, it became more difficult to balance my family with my professional life. In my son's college entrance essay, he wrote that he was proud of me for being Superintendent, but due to my busy work schedule, I wasn't there for some important times in his upbringing. He also wrote that I had a role that was bigger than any of them and that he and his sister were part of that responsibility. I feel honored that as Superintendent, I get to help the 80,000 kids in the district become educated and achieve their dreams, and every policy action I take is designed to ensure that they have every opportunity to be successful in life. As impacting as my job is, after I read the essay, I made some changes and evaluated work decisions differently. I cut my travel and only took trips which most positively impacted the district. Now when I am home, I am home. I used to bring work home with me, and now I don't. If my son calls at 7:00 p.m. and wants to go for a walk with me, I stop working when I need to and meet my son.

My greatest challenge as a father is probably the one that all fathers have, the wondering if I made the right decisions with my kids. Was I was too hard or easy on them? It all falls into perspective. I felt terrified and worried when I sent my kids off to college. I was so proud of them for exerting their independence and making sound decisions on their own. And they did really well!

I never want to sit on the sidelines in the lives of my kids. I want to be involved, active, loving them unconditionally.

I was fortunate to have a father who provided healthy modeling of being a father and man. The power of his positive impact has been far-reaching. I've gotten to pass on the love and wisdom I received to my kids, who are my greatest joy. As Superintendent, I draw on my leadership skills as a parent and my professional experience to help those I serve in the Long Beach Unified School District. I hope that my kids and the students in the District all have fulfilling lives of joy, meaning, and accomplishment.

__Today, let's use our gifts and talents to have a positive impact on those in our path.__

THE WONDER OF THE UNIVERSE

Mat Kaplan
California

J.J. – I met Mat Kaplan when I heard him give a presentation on Mars at the Long Beach Shakespeare Company prior to a remake of the 1938 War of the Worlds radio show. He spoke with such passion about Mars and space exploration, that I wanted to learn more. Since my areas of interest are the arts and humanities, I felt that anyone who could raise my enthusiasm about Mars, must be a great father if he is one. After learning that he was a dad, I interviewed him and found that he was even more passionate about being a father.

—

I love science! It was my father who planted the seeds for my lifelong passion. He gave me science books to read and took me to museums and libraries. He valued learning and taught me that its pursuit was worthy of my time, study, and energy. My father, who was a surgeon, taught my brother and me both to appreciate life and nature. He was a social, gregarious man who loved being with people. I share his same love of people and life, which carried over into my love of science and space. I later combined these affections in my professional positions. I work as a university administrator and am the Media Producer and *Planetary Radio* Host at the Planetary Society in Pasadena, CA. The Planetary Society engages in space exploration, educates the public about it, and advocates for it. Their mission is to, "create a better future by exploring other worlds and understanding our own."[4]

When I became a father, I wanted to spur my daughters on to be passionate the way my father had encouraged me. I raised them to value art and science. We went to museums, did science fair projects, and read plenty of books. I encouraged their appreciation of nature through camping trips, long hikes, and deep discussions of why things work the way they do. I remember the time my oldest daughter did a science project comparing our dog's teeth to her sister's teeth. It was such a fun way to learn about the differences between the carnivore, the dog, and the omnivore, the human. I believe being scientifically literate is more than just being educated but part of being a good citizen. I believe it's crucial for people to have a basic understanding of how the universe works in order to comprehend issues facing humanity, such as climate change, the need to conserve energy, care for the environment, and provide healthy food for those on Earth. I wanted my daughters to grasp and value this.

When the girls were young, my wife worked three nights a week teaching school, which gave me a special time alone with my daughters. I loved reading stories to them. Their favorite was *Santa Calls* by William Joyce. The main characters have a Prairie laboratory for research and experimentation; one character engages in a simple version of the scientific method; and the treacherous crime is solved by the main character's creative invention and scientific know-how. It felt like I was reading a story about my precious science-loving family.

As much as my girls love science, I also wanted them to be caring and decent people, to give to others, and to always be curious. Children are so full of wonder and have a natural curiosity about life. I think, as a father, I can help sustain that won-

[4]http://planetary.org

der or hinder it by letting opportunities pass by without using them as teaching moments. I encourage new fathers to sustain their children's sense of "the wonder of the universe." We went on camping trips and visited state and national parks which put us in the middle of nature. We hiked and learned about the environment from attending Park Rangers' Wilderness Talks on topics such as the geology, plant, and animal life of the area.

I often think back on those times when my girls were little, and we explored those wonders together. I wish I could go back in time for an hour or two… running with my daughter as she bounced upon my back in a backpack, laughing hysterically, after a hike in Yosemite. I enjoyed the great pleasure she was experiencing and feeling her so close to me on my back. I cherish the time I spend with my daughters now that they are grown, and I hope they have the same kind of joy from having children that I've had raising them. I am proud of the kind people they have become, and I enjoy seeing them succeed in their careers. My oldest daughter is an anchorperson and my youngest, an actress.

Fatherhood is truly one of the greatest wonders, and I highly recommend it. It is endlessly frustrating, terribly frightening, and more than difficult at times, but there's no question, it is the most exhilarating journey in life and by far the most important thing you'll ever do on this planet- to raise children to be good people. As proud as I am of my professional accomplishments, nothing compares to being a dad. Even if I were to travel into space, which is one of my greatest desires, being a dad would still be better. Being a father is the best thing in and out of this world!

***Today, let's notice and stand in awe of
the infinite wonders of the universe.***

INVESTING WISELY IN FAMILY

Jeff Napper
California

J.J. – I interviewed Jeff Napper at the LBS Financial Credit Union where he serves as President/CEO. For our talk, he set out framed pictures of his children at our table to celebrate his joy of being a father.

—

Family is always a safe place to come to and experience love, and it is my greatest joy in life to be a father who facilitates that kind of environment. I am honored to be the father of two adult sons and one daughter. I feel blessed to influence, shape, and mold the character of my children. My father taught me the prime importance of family and told me often how much he loved me and my siblings. My wife and I do the same with our kids. We eat dinner together and go the church on Sundays. It was harder when my kids were in high school due to their sports activities, but we maintained this practice as often as possible. We also enjoyed celebrating birthdays and holidays with our extended family.

My father instilled in me the value of education. There was no doubt that I would go to college, the only question being which college to attend. I passed the value of education onto my children who are all college graduates. They were diligent in their studies, and each finished their bachelor's degree in four years. My eldest son also graduated from law school and is now an attorney.

When my children were growing up, I had fun being involved with their sports activities. They were all on soccer teams, so during soccer season we attended three games every Saturday to cheer on our children. When my kids were in high school, they ran track and cross-country. My wife and I went to track meets for nine years to support our kids. We were team parents and organized the annual banquets. On days when my kids had meets, I left work at a designated time in order to attend. We were involved in every one of our children's extracurricular activities, went to Back-to-School nights, and anything else we could to support our kids, whether on the athletic field or in the classroom.

My role as a father has changed overtime. The transition from when they were babies, to grade school, to teenage, and now adult years, has been a process of slowly letting go each year. When my children were infants, I was more involved with caring for them physically, such as changing diapers. My kids needed less guidance as they grew. At every stage though, it's important to tell them how much they're loved, that you believe in them, and that you are proud of them.

My greatest joys are seeing my kids be happy, have integrity, stand on their own feet, and make wise decisions. On the morning of my eldest son's wedding day, he said, "It feels like I'm at the top of the stairs on Christmas morning." I live in a two-story home, and my kids' bedrooms were upstairs. On Christmas mornings when my kids were growing up, they stood at the top of the stairs and looked down at the tree and presents in great excitement about what treasures they held. I felt grateful that my eldest son compared one of the most special days of his life to the joy he experienced as a child at holiday time.

Financial management skills were important for me to pass onto my kids, which I learned from my parents. They used the envelope system, where they had an accordion file labeled with budget categories. Other than their mortgage, they put cash from each paycheck in the envelopes to cover their expenses. I taught my kids to PYF-Pay Yourself First, where they save a percentage of each paycheck. When they get a windfall, such as a bonus or tax refund, I tell them to save a certain amount of it, such as 50%, and then wisely spend or save the rest. In addition, I encourage them to give financially to such areas as their faith community.

When my kids were born, my wife and I opened two credit union accounts for them. One was for their personal savings, and the other was for education. Our names were put on the accounts with our kids. I put money in their education funds each month and later paid for their college educations.

It was crucial to teach my kids to identify between financial needs and wants. Needs, of course, being rent or mortgage, and wants such as eating at a restaurant or going to the movies. In addition, I taught them a purposeful use of credit. When my kids turned eighteen, they got a Visa credit card with a $2500 limit to be used for important needs such as college books. I told them to pay the credit card off in full every month and not abuse it. I said to be discriminatory with their purchases, so that the credit card could be a positive financial tool and help them build a strong credit rating. This is the only credit card my kids have, and they pay it off fully every month. Teaching my kids sound fiscal practices has paid off, for they are financially wise and solvent young adults.

Fatherhood takes a lot of time and energy. Some of my personal interests were put on hold until my kids became more independent. Time passes quickly, and children's growing up years cannot be regained. Although I lead a financial institution where people invest money, my greatest investment has been the time, care, support, and guidance I've given my kids. I've reaped priceless dividends from this investment! My kids are happy, healthy, responsible adults, and my family continues to nurture and celebrate our close family ties. We are bonded with the glue of love, which always goes up in value.

__Today, let's assess our financial practices and take steps to have a more manageable, peaceful, and prosperous financial life and to continue to invest wisely in our families as well.__

EDUCATION, UNITED FAMILIES, AND SIMPLICITY

Pedro Acosta
Mexico

"No education, no progress." My father's words echoed what he believed, that education was the key to having a good life and the only way to progress. It was critical, he often said, to finish college in order to have dignity and live well; and that without education, life would be more restrictive. If my siblings or I didn't receive good grades, my father told us it was our responsibility to study and perform well in school. I am proud to show the results of his efforts–I graduated with a Bachelor of Science Degree in Engineering from the University of Mexico.

As a father of a twnety-two-month-old son, I believe it's important to think about which profession is best to pursue for providing for my family. I program computers. In addition to work, I'm committed to spending time with my wife and son. When I get home from work at night and see my son, thoughts of what happened on the job, good or bad, fade away. On weekends, we take our son to the park where he enjoys watching the dogs play and other park activities. I also bathe my son and wash his hair while I shower. When it's time to change my son's diapers, I sing a song to him first in Spanish, then in English, which begins, "Let's go change diapers." He loves when I sing this song to him!

I love raising a child and am amazed at the mystery of reproduction which produces such a wonderful being. Since my boy is still young, he wakes up several times during the night. My sleep and energy levels are often low, so I must prioritize my time. I'd like to have some time in between having another child. Being a parent is extremely hard work! When my son was nine-months-old, he wanted to walk. It was difficult bending over to help him walk after sitting at work all day. Fathers have to "bend" literally and figuratively to be flexible with their children's needs and natural desires. I work to learn what his generation thinks to help me understand the times in which he'll grow up, so that I can be flexible there, too.

From being a father, I've learned that life is full of happiness, but you have to find your own happiness. I view the family unit as a circle and believe it's highly important for the husband, wife, and children to stay together in order to keep the circle complete. Family members must give their best effort to stay united, for if they don't, all lose out. I see so many children without fathers, and my heart breaks watching them.

Children don't always understand why their father isn't there. It's hard to have a full view of life, which children receive from having both parents living in the home, when a parent is missing. I have a sister who is a single mother, and others tease her son at school for not having a father at home. I counsel my nephew to let the cruel comments roll off him and dismiss them from his mind and heart. I tell him to not respond to the teasing with sarcastic comments, it will just bring more cruelty from the other kids.

Life is full of challenges, and busyness adds to this. I believe living a simple life is of great value because it gives families more quiet time and opportunity to be together. It's hard when people become burdened by a lot of debt and have to work longer hours away from family to pay that off. I have monthly car and rent payments. I earn a good income, but feeling pressured

EDUCATION, UNITED FAMILIES, AND SIMPLICITY

by the expenses, and owing money makes life harder. If you can live with just what is necessary, you will be happier.

> *J.J. – At the close of our interview, I told Pedro that I wanted a simpler life, and he told me that I may need to move from Los Angeles County to Montgomery, Alabama, where the movie character, Forrest Gump, lived. Although I didn't move, Pedro's guidance has helped me live in a more relaxed and intentional manner.*

Today, let's live simply and spend our time on the essentials in our lives.

8

RESPECT

*"I told my daughters that
the best and most desirable trait
in boys is respect for girls."*

✥

Eluid Martinez, Ph.D.

CELEBRATING DAUGHTERS

Eliud Martinez, Ph.D.
California

Nothing in my life can compare with the joy of seeing my daughters being born. The image is vivid in my memory. I see my wife and myself in the delivery room. Holding my wife's hand, I look over her shoulder, across her abdomen swollen with pulsating life and gaze into a mirror placed in front of her. I see a tiny head emerge gradually, then an arm poke free, then another. The doctor reaches under the baby's arms. As the baby emerges belly down, the doctor lifts up the infant, dangling legs, back and buttocks all wet and shiny with amniotic fluid, still connected to the life-giving umbilical cord. Then the doctor turns the baby around for us to see (we did not know the sex in advance in those days) and says, "It's a girl!"

The doctor and nurses cut the umbilical cord, drain the newborn infant's nostrils, put eye drops in her eyes, wipe away some amniotic fluid, and place the wet, tiny baby in my arms. Now for the rest of my life, I will know the joy of holding my newborn infant in my arms and the strength and tenderness the infant brings forth from the heart. It's the breathtaking, deeply emotional experience of becoming a father.

Being an artist, I gazed in awe at the baby in my arms. My wife and I have created this precious creature. I marveled at the perfection of the shapes of the ears, tiny nose and nostrils, lips and chin. The infant seemed weightless, and a powerful sense of protectiveness, pride, and tenderness swept over me. I felt the warm, bare, tender skin on my arms and softness of the face. I examined the baby further. Two perfect little arms; tiny, chubby hands with perfect fingers and fingernails; two equally perfect legs, feet, toes and toenails; and the magical cleft of womanhood where nature placed it.

As my daughters grew up, I saw my role much as I see my role as a university professor: as a guide. I looked into my daughters' hearts and minds for what learning and play activities brought joy, compassion, and self-understanding. I praised curiosity, imagination, friendship, and goodwill. I encouraged independence in carrying out tasks, reminding them that I'd be delighted to help, if needed. I told my daughters that the best and most desirable trait in boys is respect for girls.

When my daughters were young, one or the other sister often had a friend over to play. If competition developed between the sisters for the visitor's friendship, I said that if the three couldn't play nicely, I could not permit them the privilege of having a friend visit. That usually ended the unpleasantness, and I told them that most friendships are temporary, but sisters are forever.

Perhaps the most vivid memory of my daughters is rushing out of the room whenever I had to spank either of them, because it used to make me cry. I was very relieved when their mother suggested that we should stop spanking the girls. They were too big now for that, she had said, seven and nine, if I remember correctly. We agreed that from then on, the girls could be punished simply by separating them and banishing them to their rooms, which were their sanctuaries.

Another memory from among numerous others is when I removed the training wheels from my youngest daughter's bicycle. She wanted me to hold the bicycle and run alongside of her until she could ride it alone. My thoughts become so vivid as I see myself letting go of the bicycle. There she goes, my sweetheart, mi corazoncito, mi preciosa.

I also remember her singing in the shower, walking on her hands, the piano composition that she wrote when she was eleven or twelve, promising me grandchildren one day. And now at the age of forty-three, on the eleventh of September of this year (2013), she has given me a grandson, named after a famous musical genius.

I am immensely grateful for my wife and daughters. Without them, my life would have been very different, and perhaps much shorter. My daughters have taught me to appreciate the joys and intimacies of family life. Fatherhood has permitted me to see, to know and to understand the complete cycle of human life: from my daughters' birth, through every season of a woman's magical life, to maturity in my own life with my wife.

Because of the close relationship with my wife and daughters, I was also blessed to know the day when each of my girls crossed the bridge of puberty to the enchanted land of womanhood. Their mother and I had prepared them. After many trips to the bathroom one day, our eldest daughter came and said, *"Dad, it came."* On my younger daughter's day, her mother said, "Tell Dad that now there are three women in this house." She did, and I was deeply moved by the grandeur of human life, the miracle of procreation. "Maybe one day," I thought, "I will be a grandfather." Now that I am, my heart is filled with infinite gratitude and emotional fulfillment. As the song says, "Thank Heaven for little girls…"

***Today, let's acknowledge and
celebrate the feminine side in us all.***

LONG-DISTANCE FATHERHOOD

Nacho Ariza
Spain

It's difficult to be a dad who is away most of the time from his family. I'm in the Air Force and work in Munich, Germany, on a NATO project with others from Spain, Italy, Germany, and the United Kingdom. We work in the Contracting Department on a fighter plane. Working with people from several countries has taught me about a variety of cultures. Our common purpose in working for NATO supersedes any of our cultural differences though, and the deeper bond of our shared humanity and efforts to promote international peace, unites us all.

Being in the military, I followed in my father's footsteps. He was in the Spanish Air Force. He taught me to love and be loved. He instilled an appreciation of family and home in me, as well as the importance of being close to those you love. It grieves me, being away from my family, yet I know what I do matters and supports them, as I work from abroad.

I have a twenty-one-year-old daughter who is studying to be a pharmacist at the University in Madrid. The day my daughter was born was the best day of my life. My father-in-law is a doctor, and I watched my daughter's birth at his home in Málaga.

Being a father is the most important thing in my life. There is no greater act of love in all creation than to bring a new life into being. I teach my daughter to love, be honest, and respect others. I never realized until after I became a father, that I hadn't said, "I love you" very often to my parents. I regret that and tell my daughter that I love her every chance I get. I want the best for her future and happiness. She now has a steady boyfriend, and it's hard for me to let her become independent. I admit that I feel jealous because of the time she spends with him. Someday she'll marry, create a new home with the family she'll bring into the world, and live away from my wife and me. I know that this is normal, and I did it at the same age. I will rejoice as she matures into adulthood, but I also mourn this "letting go." I anticipate crying on her wedding day because I'll be so proud of her growth and new life.

Although it's been difficult for me in Germany, I think it's good for a person to have the opportunity to live abroad for a short period of time before getting married. It's a chance to experience a new lifestyle, practice a second language, and gain skills in independence. I cope with my time abroad by talking to my wife daily on the phone, being active in my life in Germany, and being friends with a fellow Spaniard in the same situation as me. It also seems the farther away I am from my family, the tighter bonds I have with them become. Though I miss them dearly, I reflect more deeply on how much I value them.

Today, let's tell and show someone we love them, whether close or far away.

HABITAT FOR HUMANITY

David Howard
California

    I grew up in a household filled with pain, abuse, and dysfunction. It lacked the kindness that all humans deserve. Several family members molested me. These experiences hurt me and damaged my self-esteem and sense of self. I drank excessively to cope with the pain. However, I became determined to survive and overcome my background. I got sober and created a new life based on giving to others. I worked privately as a building contractor and also for Habitat for Humanity as a vocation and avocation. I believe in their mission, which is to build affordable housing for low-income families in need with interest-free loans. The money the families pay goes into a revolving fund to build homes for other families. All families in the program become part of building their home and others' homes. I have built homes for families in thirty-eight countries and continue in my efforts. One time, I served on the Habitat for Humanity team which built 1,000 homes in Durban, South Africa, on land donated by Nelson Mandela.

    When I became a father, I stopped the cycle of pain and created a humane habitat and upbringing for my daughter, now fourteen. I am grateful for the opportunity to raise her differently than what I experienced.

    When my daughter was five, I became a single father. Although my ex-wife and I were not compatible marriage partners, we are compatible co-parents and have 50/50 custody. Typically, my daughter stays half the week at her mother's and half at my home. We have duplicates of everything to help our daughter transition back and forth between our homes. She has double sets of clothes and the same furniture in each of her bedrooms. We eat dinner at the same time in both households and keep her activity levels the same for her studies and sports schedule. This gives my daughter continuity and strong support from my ex-wife and me. Currently, my ex-wife rents a room in my home, which helps our daughter since she doesn't need to move back and forth during the week.

I teach my daughter to know who she is, to express herself, and accept only true friends. I hope that she will identify and develop her talents, find her own spiritual faith, and follow her intuition in life. I am concerned about how her friends are influencing her. I hope that she will be fearless and stay true to herself and not change who she is to fit in with the "popular crowd" at school. I have enjoyed watching her evolve from the awkward "tweens" into a loving, passionate adolescent who is involved in school activities and gives to others. At her high school she is in the Pink Club, a club which has fundraisers and disperses information on breast cancer. Their motto is, "Check yourself or wreck yourself."

Letting go as a parent has had challenges though. One time, my daughter and some of her friends were accosted at an amusement park. They were locked in a store at the park until Security freed them. My instinct as a protector was to jump in and save them. I wanted to empower my daughter though, so I asked her how she wanted to handle the situation. She wanted the perpetrators found and identified. I also filed a police report and gave her the support and professional counseling to heal. Although I helped her deal with the trauma, I let her have her own voice and sense of control in resolving and overcoming it.

Fatherhood can be stressful. I would tell myself, "It gets better after six months." When my daughter was a toddler, we sang this song together. I said, "You're my little bit, and I love you so." She responded, "Much!" Then in unison, we sang, "That's right!" Then we would both burst out laughing. I love being a dad. It's my favorite thing in the world.

> *J.J. – When I interviewed David, I wondered if his comments as a single father would differ from those of married fathers. They did not. A dad is a dad. The caring heart and loving, generous spirit of a father prevails whether he is married or not. In fact, David got teary-eyed when he expressed his gratitude for being a father and his great love for his daughter.*

Today, let's be "construction workers" and say words of encouragement to build others up and "construct" more human beings filled with self-esteem and self-respect.

"MARRY A GOOD MOTHER"
Excerpts from Ed Sewell's Letter to His Children

Ed Sewell, Ed.D.
California

Dear Kids,

    A father's wisdom number one for you, Cliff and Travis, is to marry a good mother; and Stacy, to continue to be the good mother that you are. "Mothering" reminds me of our 1996 trip to the United Kingdom. We toured with a group of Australians visiting castles, churches, manor houses, ad infinitum. One morning, we explored Hadrian's Wall. After thirty minutes, Colin, a retired Aussie sheepman, noticed a flock of sheep and their shepherd in an adjacent field. Having learned more about Hadrian than he wanted to know, Colin scrambled over a rock fence and approached the shepherd. Several Australians and I followed him into the muddy field. We exchanged pleasantries in three different accents, but I'll never forget Colin asking the shepherd, "Good mothers are they?" Quality mothering is the bedrock of any family.

    You have been blessed with such a mother; pass on your experience to your children. The environment that you provide for them, especially in the early years, is critical, and there is no better environmentalist than a good mother.

    Remember your early childhood. Mother was a constant for you both, Cliff and Travis. Stacy, your mother and I tag-teamed you because we both worked during the early years of our marriage. Travis, your weekly trips to speech therapy and the follow-up drills were the direct result of M.O.M. (mother-on-mission). Your admission to Duke University and law school, as well as your career as a deputy district attorney, can be correlated to a determined mother. Perhaps one anecdote involving you, Cliff, as a toddler will reinforce the value of a loving, caring mother. While playing in the backyard you could entertain yourself quite well, but every thirty minutes or so you would toddle to the door and yell, "Maw," in a loud voice. As soon as your mother answered, you resumed your play. Maw was there, and all was well.

If possible, avoid institutional child care, especially for the first three years of your children's lives, just as you've avoided commercial kennel care for your puppies. Your career and personal pleasures may have to take a back seat for a while. Scheduling will be a constant juggle, but is not the most critical developmental period in your baby's life worth the effort? Rick and Stacy, because of occupational vagaries, you were able to dodge regular childcare; perhaps an omniscient force intervened in the form of layoffs and career change. If that be so, your mother, Glenda, and I thank fate for assisting in the development of two happy, confident grandchildren.

Happenstance did not control your early years. Your mother subordinated any thought of a career. Nurturing our children became her life's work. While I taught day and night, coached, pursued a doctorate, and began an apartment business, mom focused on you. Money was in short supply, so she began a backyard preschool. Added to caring for you three were one or two teachers' children. She only accepted teachers' kids to protect our family vacations.

Childcare-by-Glenda was unorthodox and, at times, perhaps unsanitary. One of my teaching colleagues recalled picking her daughter up one afternoon. She entered the backyard and was horrified to see five dirty kids, clad only in underwear,

"MARRY A GOOD MOTHER"

chasing the rabbit, annoying the turtle, playing in the always present mudhole, or re-washing an unhappy dog.

Co-mingled with the chaos were frequent trips to the park, beach, nearby field, and library. I'm sure that the librarian was relieved to see Glenda et al. depart, but the crew always left, books-in-hand. Your mom's daycare had two slender threads of organization: storytime and snack time. It wasn't unusual to observe four to six dirty kids, clustered around mom listening to a *Curious George* story while eating a banana. Tattered copies of *Blaze, Curious George*, and other childhood artifacts rest in your mother's cedar chest. Cliff and Travis, someday you may want to revive and reuse them–your sister did.

Over the years, many teacher-mothers entrusted their children to Glenda and were universal in their gratitude for her surrogate mothering. There was always a waiting list for Childcare-by-Glenda.

Your mother's quality mothering has continued throughout your lives to adulthood. Wise fathers would agree: Give your kids the best–a good mother.

Today, let's thank our mothers, whether living or having passed away, for the gift of life.

9

SERVICE

"My vision is for people to live in peace and diversity where they respect every living thing because the Earth is our home."

✣

Julio Olalla

A MAN OF SERVICE

Abdullah Akbar
Afghanistan/California

I was born in Kabul, Afghanistan, the youngest of ten children. My father loved the United States and would often read American novels to my brothers, sisters and me. We especially loved the spy stories he read to us. I looked forward to when he would finish a new book because then he would read it to us. Those were good times. Unfortunately, when I was twelve years old, my father unexpectedly died of a heart attack at the age of sixty-two. This was disastrous to our family because he had been our leader. I was able to continue schooling, though, and receive my Bachelor's Degree. In 1970, at age twenty-one, I obtained a visa, and with only $1,300 in my pocket, I came to New York. I wish my father had been able to see me fulfill my dream- the dream he fueled and helped build in me, of coming to the United States.

American society was extremely different from life in Afghanistan. I often wrote my family that it was the land of opportunity where a person could be anything he or she wanted to be. I learned English and studied business. I managed a theater on Broadway and lived with the Jewish family of a friend I had met in college. Though our faiths differed, they never hindered our friendship, and we even joked about it. This family became so precious to me.

I felt the loss of my father but not the absence of the wisdom and life lessons he had passed onto me. He was a devout Muslim who read the *Koran* and prayed every morning and throughout the day. He lived the principles of Islam such as service, generosity, and gratitude for one's blessings. I follow his example.

My parents met each other near a holy site, when my father was in the military. They both were on horseback, and as she turned to avoid some mud, her veil dropped, revealing just a glimpse of her face. It was at that moment my father fell deeply in love with her. He returned home and told his father he must marry this woman. It was against tribal customs to marry outside one's tribe, and she was not of his tribe. My father's great love persisted, and he eventually returned to Western Afghanistan where he asked my mother to marry him. She was a tender sixteen years old. They had a deeply committed and wonderful marriage. My father greatly valued my mother and taught me to support women. He recognized that although he provided the income, my mother ran the household affairs. He was generous with women and loved buying gifts for my sisters. When he returned from vacations, he hid gifts, like jewels and silken materials, in their rooms. He was such a giving and caring man. He cut our hair, sewed our clothes, and fixed our shoes. And this from such a humble man who was once a general in the Afghan army and an advisor to the Afghan king!

In 1979, the Soviet Union invaded Afghanistan, and within a short time, one of my brothers and three of my cousins were killed. One of the basic Muslim tenets is to be of service and help those in need. My father had instilled this in me. I had attained prosperity in the United States and felt called to be of service and help my country. I went to Pakistan and joined the resistance, the Mujahideen. The CIA learned that I spoke perfect English, so after helping my family come to the U.S., I returned to Pakistan to work for the CIA as an undercover operative. Overtime, I got discouraged. In time it was no longer a 'Holy War' against the infidels, the Soviets, but a mad existence of corruption, treachery, drugs and jewels, and even betrayal against my own people.[5] The puppet leadership offered me a position, but after learning about their corrupt practices, I declined and returned to the U.S. My father taught me to have the highest standards of integrity and morals, and I could not accept such corruption.

I think of my father often, and now that I have a son and two daughters, I want to pass on his legacy. I tell them stories about what life was like in Afghanistan when I grew up. I know they have experienced so much freedom and abundance by being born in the U.S. But with that freedom comes a lot of responsibility, and I want my children to use this freedom in a healthy way. In order to help them be grateful for what they have, I subscribe to *The Smithsonian* and *National Geographic* magazines, and I read the *Los Angeles Times* and *Orange County Register* daily. I give my kids articles from these publications to learn about other areas that I believe are important. I then ask them questions about the articles to check their understanding. We also watch documentaries because many charities make films about countries they are helping, and my children learn about the core problems these countries face, such as needing medical supplies, vaccinations, and educational aid.

It is very important to me that my children learn to be tolerant of people of all faiths. I belong to an organization called Christians and Muslims for Peace (CAMP), which meets once a month. People of different faiths attend to create more peaceful ties between us all. When I came to the U.S. and lived in a Jewish home, I received a lot of love. One time, the family even canceled a vacation because I couldn't get off work that weekend. The *Koran* contains information about tolerance, and

[5]Image Magazine, September-October 2002 Issue, P. 49

when I read it, I take notes on tolerance. I then discuss the notes with my children. Fanatics are dangerous because they divide people, who are brothers and sisters under one God, thus creating hatred between them. In the Old and New Testaments, God said that false messengers would be known by their fruits. People like Bin Laden are dangerous fanatics whose fruits are deadly.

My role as a father is critical because a father impacts everything in his family such as the way everyone walks, sleeps, speaks, and works. It's my responsibility to protect my children and provide the best environment for their upbringing. When my youngest daughter was a baby, her favorite place to fall asleep was on my chest. If she had difficulty falling asleep, I leaned on my side, and my wife put her on my chest. She then fell asleep within minutes, for my heartbeat soothed her to sleep. She knew she was safe nestled near my heart.

My greatest fear as a father has been of not raising good children or not being a positive influence on them. I have discussed this with them to help them understand how I feel. I am grateful that my children have turned out well, and my greatest joy is seeing their success. Sometimes when I look at my children, I can't take my eyes off them. I simply enjoy looking at them. I even close my eyes at times and imagine what I want for them. I see them acting their best and having good lives. I am proud that they are productive and contribute in society. My children have also taught me, and I live a healthier life because of them. When they were little, I smoked. They did not like this and put up a, "No Smoking" sign in our home. I quit smoking.

Being involved with my children from the start meant everything to me: I changed diapers and put each one to bed. If a father is involved with his children from the beginning, they won't withdraw from him later. I see no separation of duties between men and women in parenting. Both parents should be involved with every aspect of raising their children. It's also important how people parent, because children learn how to be parents from them.

God has blessed me with much goodness, but I have learned that satisfaction in life is not in wealth, power, influence, knowledge, or intelligence. My greatest joy and satisfaction is my family. I am content with my life because I've seen the other side of it.

J.J. – After Abdullah shared these tender memories with me, he stretched out on a booth in his restaurant to show me how he used to lie on his side when his daughter fell asleep on his chest. I felt privileged to witness what felt like a sacred act of love by this caring father and man of service.

Today, let's be of service and bring whatever joy we can to our fellows.

THE GIFT OF BEING THERE

Congressman Alan Lowenthal
California

J.J. – When I called Congressman Lowenthal's office in Long Beach to request the interview, I was impressed that he set aside time in his busy schedule to talk about fatherhood. This showed me the high value he places on family.

When I met him in person, I experienced a man who loves his kids, is their friend and parent, and who carries the same commitment of being there and working hard for the needs, issues, and concerns of his constituents. I am grateful and fortunate to live in the district of a Congressman who is so highly dedicated to being there for his family and community.

—

As a father, I focused on spending time with my sons and developing quality relationships with them. I coached my sons' soccer and baseball teams and supported their educational pursuits. When I became a university professor, I balanced my time between my family and professional responsibilities. I took two sabbaticals where our family spent a year abroad, each time in different countries. My sons grew educationally from these experiences, and our family became closer. Now that I am a grandfather, I remain close and active with my family. Recently I took my two granddaughters trick- or-treating for Halloween.

We had a great time as well on a recent trip to the local pumpkin patch!

My children always know that I am there for them, to help them deal with various challenges in life. I listen, spend the time, and provide a safe place for them to relax and share their thoughts and feelings. I lend an understanding ear, without judgment, and I offer my sons unconditional positive regard to support them in the various stages of their lives.

I would advise new fathers to enjoy their children and share as much time with them as possible. I'd tell them to appreciate their kids, for time passes quickly, so it's important to set aside and value special times together.

I am just as committed to being there for people in my community. I've served my community for many years in City Council, the State Assembly, State Senate, and now Congress. I modeled and encouraged my sons to be politically aware and active and to give back to their community as well. My sons now have professions where they are of service to the public. Parents can foster civic responsibilities in their children if they are politically aware, contributing to their community, and exposing their children to such knowledge and practices. As a Congressman, I am honored to be of service to the residents in my district. I also raised my sons to have the same dedicated mindset.

Today, let's give the gift of being there in time, full attention, and sincerity of heart for those in our personal and professional circles.

EMBRACING NEW WAYS OF THINKING, SEEING, AND LIVING

Julio Olalla
Chile and United States

My upbringing was quite different than the lives my children have experienced. My father came to Chile as a Spanish refugee in 1937, during the last year of the Civil War there. I left Chile in 1973, and went to Argentina and then on to the United States as a refugee because of the political turmoil in Chile. From my own and my father's experiences as refugees, I learned a greater appreciation of life.

When I came to the U.S., I questioned everything that I believed. I realized that I had received a digested world view and was not thinking freely. I studied the philosophy of language and learned through my studies to observe my thoughts and to have a greater awareness and experience of myself, others, and life. I want to pass this on to my family.

I am the father of two generations of children. I have two grown daughters in their twenties and an energetic two-year-old son. I am a different father at my current age of fifty-four than when I raised my daughters when I was in my twenties. Back then, I felt the pressure of teaching them as much as I could. I had a lot more rules and fears. Today, I trust in the unfolding of my beautiful child. I am less concerned with providing my son with knowledge than with giving him a strong emotional foundation.

The best gift I can give my son is for him be able to experience what I have learned from life and feel the full range of emotions including joy, sadness, and gratitude. I freely show him the joy I feel that he is a part of my life and my gratitude for his existence; this instills confidence in him. People must learn this experientially, not just by looking it up on the Internet. In this technological world, people are so concerned with *learning* information, that they've forgotten that wisdom is not the product of information. So I thank my son, and he in turn thanks me for things. Recently, we were in the countryside and saw the full, beautiful moon rising over a hill. My wife said that she was grateful to see the beautiful scene, and my son chimed in, "Tell the moon you are grateful." I was delighted to see that my son was grasping this concept of gratitude.

My little boy loves building and taking things a part, such as his own playpen! He loves smelling the flowers and catching insects in the garden. He delights in the stories I tell him. Children just seem to know how to play and rest and learn from it all. I believe that the purest source of learning is play. I enjoy playing at every opportunity with my son, and we play a lot, physically. My daughters played in a softer, more affectionate way. We could learn so much from children if we took time to play as adults. The joy I see in my son makes me think he is so much wiser that I am.

My son is attentive to the world in a particular way, and this helps me see the world anew with the curious, attentive eye of a child. One day, we removed a huge spider from the swimming pool. My son asked, "Why did the spider fall into the spout?" To me, the spider was a small detail I may never have concerned myself with at all. I replied that the spider was trying to get a drink. He then asked why the spider was trying to drink. The endless questions of a two-year-old! At the end of our talk, I realized that my son was more interested in being in the conversation where he was heard, answered, and attended to, than in the actual content of the conversation.

I take my son seriously by answering his questions with respect and patience so that he learns that he is valuable. Children love to ask questions and they take everything in stride. They love simplicity. This is a state of total freedom. The innocent tenderness of children is a breath of fresh air!

My desire is that all people live simply, like a child, in peace, where they respect every living thing because the Earth is our home. I hope people will accept that we all see the world differently and respect that. I pass this view onto my children. I encourage them to develop their insights and gifts. I ask them, "What will you offer others from the bottom of your soul?" After one of my daughters finished college, she lived one year at home. During this time, she learned that her gift was an ability to heal. She liked acupuncture the most and enrolled in a school of acupuncture. She is now a dedicated acupuncturist serving her patients.

Once in a while, we need to look at a star and be in touch with the immensity of the universe and get a sense of humility. We've stopped looking at the sky. It is so worthwhile to look up. In Chile and the U.S., one has to go into the country to see the stars since pollution covers them in the cities. Gazing at the vastness of the universe helps us realize we are all tiny, yet valuable parts of this creation. Hopefully, someday, our part of the universe will live together in love, peace, and harmony with respect and gratitude for all.

Today, let's live in gratitude and allow ourselves to feel the fullness of life.

TRAVEL, TALK AND CHOICE

Eric Jul, Ph.D.
Denmark

"It's 9:00 p.m., come have some tea." Six to seven nights a week, my family and I have dinner together and then do our own thing, but at 9:00 p.m., we gather on the sofa, talk, and have a cup of tea. We discuss the current issues of the day, what tomorrow holds for us, and any problems we may be facing. We don't watch much television. I place a high value on talking with my family. I believe we bond through such communication.

I also believe that travel communicates things that words cannot express. I have made it a priority to travel extensively with my children. Traveling is the best education. My family and I have trekked across Denmark, Norway, and Austria, breathing in such sites as cathedrals, art museums, and memorial grounds. We would visit one cultural site a day and then discuss it. We've endured long car trips through France and Germany, talking to people as we went, learning about them and their beliefs. My children have gained a cultural richness, and when they study artworks and historical sites in school, they appreciate and relate to them better because they've seen many of them first-hand.

My father taught me that people should be free to make their own choices, and I give my kids this freedom also. I teach them to evaluate the advantages and disadvantages of a decision and then to take responsibility for their choice. When we are skiing, I might ask, "Would you like to have lunch now?" Then they might answer, "No, we'd like to ski." I give my kids opportunities to decide so that they feel a part of the planning. Some decisions come quickly, and others come after more discussion. When evaluating drinking alcohol, I tell my kids to consider their limits and the consequences, for excessive drinking leads to feeling poorly and has other harmful effects.

In the spirit of making conscientious choices, I would advise men who are considering fatherhood to carefully evaluate whether the time is right to have kids and if they are prepared for the responsibilities of being a parent. I know I have given my whole heart to the job of father.

As a father, my greatest joy is watching my kids grow up and become responsible adults; and our travels, talks, and freedom of choice helps to bring that about.

Today, let's take time to talk with one another, visit someplace new, meet new people, and learn new things.

10

PATIENCE

"Some say that it takes a village to raise children,
but with seventy-two offspring—
I raised a village!"

✢

William Jeffers, Jr.

FATHER OF TEN

William Jeffers, Jr.
Colorado

J.J.—Special thanks to Gregory Jeffers for interviewing his father, William, while visiting him for Thanksgiving 2013. I also included Gregory's comments about his father and family.

—

I grew up during tough times in the United States. I was born in 1930 in North Platte, Nebraska, just after the Stock Market crash and at the beginning of the Great Depression. My father worked at the Railroad Roadhouse servicing trains, which was a good thing at that time as many farmers struggled in the Midwest because of the dust storms that wreaked havoc on crops. North Platte had a population of about 12,000, consisting mostly of those who worked for the railroad like my dad.

My father was a hard worker, and he taught me to work hard as well. He used to wear bib overalls and a jacket to protect himself from all the ash and soot of the trains, just like you see in the old pictures of railroad workers. Dad was a fair, honest man, and he left an impression on me to be the same—and to defend the weak and helpless. He never let anyone push him around. He had a strong sense of fairness and a great respect for women, which he passed onto me.

When I became a father, I had ten children! In order to manage such a large household, my wife and I assigned our kids chores which we wrote on a blackboard. No child was too little to do a job of some kind, which we rotated regularly. We didn't have a dishwasher in the house until the 1970s, so we washed dishes the old fashioned way: one child washed while another one dried. My kids received a weekly allowance ($.10 times their age) until they got a job of their own; then they no longer had to do chores, but they had to keep their room clean. If my kids were in trouble at school, they were also in trouble at home. This is how my dad taught me to respect authority, and I followed suit with my kids.

I love my big family, and it was such fun watching them all grow up. I would wrestle with my kids; well, it was more like a gang wrestle than one-on-one, whenever I got home. We had family picnics and played backyard games. In the winter, we shoveled snow. Even when snow was wet and heavy, I loved shoveling side by side with my kids. I remember driving my older boys around in our truck to collect papers for recycling and to earn spending money. We were green before green was in!

When my kids were grown, I loved attending their graduations and weddings–lots of weddings! I'm grateful to have raised healthy kids and to have shared a good life with them and my wife of sixty-three years, who is my greatest joy.

My most difficult challenge as a father was balancing my job as a traveling auditor with time at home. When I first started, I had a large territory to cover, and there were no cell phones, so phone calls were expensive. I had to be onsite until the job was done, which could take weeks or months. But when I was home, I was home. I didn't go out, play golf, or take any work home with me. I was there for my family. My company eventually changed their policy, and I was able come home on weekends. It was like a honeymoon started every Friday night!

Bringing up kids is challenging let alone having ten children with different genders and personalities. My wife made the house rules, and I enforced them. We faced trying times and hard decisions. Once, two of our sons let peer pressure get the best of them, and we asked them leave home due to intolerable behavior. Both my sons returned after learning a valuable lesson. They realized that living with someone else was not any better and was actually worse than living at home.

I play so many roles as a father. I am my children's protector, teacher, provider, and role model. I taught them what is right and wrong and to treat others with dignity, respect, and equality. I prepared them to face life's challenges, ups and downs. I taught my boys to look out for their neighbors and to help an elderly woman who lived across the street. Whenever it snowed, it was my sons' job to make sure her sidewalks were shoveled and to never accept any pay for it. I also taught my kids the value of working hard. I encouraged my kids to be of service, and I modeled this for them by calling Bingo at our church every Saturday for nearly thirty years to help raise money. We went to church each Sunday as a family. I would often remind my children that freedom isn't free; don't take it for granted, and fight for it if necessary.

I have learned to always treat my children fairly and with respect. I think this can be done without being a pushover. Fatherhood shouldn't be intimidating. Kids need discipline to teach them to obey the laws. I was a teaching father first and a friend second. I raised ten wonderful children and now have thirty-two grandchildren and thirty great-grandchildren. Some say that it takes a village to raise children, but with seventy-two offspring, I raised a village!

I am very proud of my kids and of who they have become. They have all pursued their talents and interests with a diverse and impressive list of professions including: a doctor, electric power plant supervisor, fire squadron captain, Caterpillar equipment repair supervisor, YMCA exercise instructor, artist/musician, construction company owner, recreational therapy consultant, procurement manager, and school teacher. We had this saying on the wall of our house, "From Roots to Wings," meaning that my wife and I gave our children the roots, and it was up to them to spread their wings. I am proud that all my children have spread their wings. I gave them the freedom to be who they are and pursue the lives which they chose.

Today, let's be the roots for children that they might spread their wings and fly!

ONE OF THE TEN

Gregory Jeffers
California

Growing up in a family of ten, we had countless nights of playing Kick the Can, Red Rover, Kickball, Capture the Flag, and Fox and Geese. Our home was never short on activities, fair or foul weather. Inside we played cards, Scrabble, Probe, Password, Monopoly, and other board games. If that was boring, we worked on a jigsaw puzzle, played ping- pong, or football. All the neighbors wanted to be a part of our household! Peace and quiet was in short supply though, and sometimes when I was little, I hid in the clothes barrel in our basement as my secret quiet place. My siblings and I also did chores and homework and could watch up to two hours of television a night. We were disciplined if needed, and sometimes we were all punished if somebody did something wrong and didn't confess. I never saw my father or mother lose their temper, aside from an occasional outburst of frustration.

When my father was younger, he was a strong oak: sturdy, unbending, protective, and deeply rooted. Some of the branches were so brittle that they broke off. He realized that those branches were not beneficial to protecting his family, and as a result, they never grew back. His trunk stayed strong though, and protection from the world for all in his family tree remains a priority to this day.

My father is now eighty-three years old and merits the highest praise. He is dedicated, trustworthy, responsible, steadfast, humble, morally sound and wise, and as strong as an ox.

He is the best example of a man I've seen in my life. He has made me into a man I can look at every day in the mirror and smile at what I see.

> ***Today, let's thank those who gave us roots and spread our wings and fly.***

"TO LOVE AND BE LOVED"

Joe Riddick
California

"The greatest thing you'll ever learn is just
to love and be loved in return."
(Lyrics from Nature Boy by Eden Ahbez)

My parents taught me to love through sharing and being considerate of others. Growing up my older sister had some health challenges. She was a beautifully talented musician. My father was a professional piano player and organist, and my mother was a gifted vocalist. Musical ability seemed to run in my family. My talents and interests, however, were in athletics, such as track and aquatics, and at times I felt less valued since I didn't pursue music.

I remember getting in trouble for something, and my father disciplined me by giving me a timeout in my bedroom. Sitting there alone, I had time to feel sorry for myself and slighted for not receiving more attention. I protested by climbing out of the window and going to a nearby park. It wasn't long before my father came looking for me. There I was sitting cross-legged on the grass in the middle of the park. He sat down with me, and we talked the whole thing out. He knew it was hard to be in my situation, but he also knew that there would be times that I wouldn't be able to do the things I wanted. We were a family, and all of our actions affected one another. I learned a lot about love and acceptance that day.

After attending college, I served two years as an officer in the Naval Reserves. I was in charge of a group of enlisted men, and this leadership training helped prepare me for being a parent. If my enlisted men did not perform their duties, I helped guide them back to the right path. There were occasions when a few of the men didn't get back to the ship at the designated time after being on shore. I saw them just like me, protesting my dad, climbing out of the window and sitting in the park. Taking a cue from Dad, I discussed options, such as why it was best to not repeat such behavior due to the negative consequences which would follow and how this affected the rest of the unit. When my enlisted men later appeared in military court for their unacceptable behavior, I offered support and guidance.

After the Navy, I worked as a high school teacher, coach and counselor. In all these positions, I used the same approach when one of my students did not follow the rules or accept their responsibilities. I talked to them about the consequences which would ensue if the behavior was repeated and helped them realize their priorities and bring them back to a responsible path.

As a father, I found great joy watching my sons mature and become responsible adults. I enjoyed watching them grow up, venturing out in athletic events such as sailing competitions, and social situations like going on a first date and to the senior prom. It's hard to imagine, but I am now a proud grandfather! I love seeing my two-year-old granddaughter explore the world, learn to talk, and have fun dancing and sailing. She reaches out her arms toward my wife and me knowing that we are there for her when she needs us. I'm blessed to offer her my love and give her that sense of security which all kids need. Soon we will have a new grandchild in the family. I am excited to offer this little one the same love and support.

Several years ago, I was severely injured in a car accident. Determined to survive and overcome, I worked hard to recover,

"TO LOVE AND BE LOVED"

and I continue to do the exercises needed for my rehabilitation. I'm grateful to live in a beautiful home just footsteps from the beach. I watch the tides go in and out at different times of the year, reminding me that I, too, must adjust and flow with the various tides in my life. The words to this song like the tides, ebb and flow in my mind, "The greatest thing you'll ever learn is just to love and be loved in return." I know that there will be challenges to come, but I will face them with love.

J.J.–Joe then showed me some of his sons' yearbooks and other cherished family photos displayed in his living room. His smile then widened, and he said, "The joy of being a father! And the unexpected joy of being a grandfather." His joy is seen in his smile, and his love is seen in his actions. May we all learn the lesson which Joe lives naturally of loving and being loved.

Today, let's give the smile of love to all who cross our path.

LOVE AND ACCEPTANCE

George Alp
California

I have come to the conclusion that the only way to teach my children is by being an example to them—*showing* them love, caring, and self-respect. There is a reason it is called, "role modeling." I was born during the Depression, and my father was extremely busy working two jobs to support our family. He taught me strong morals, to work hard, and treat others with respect. But he also turned to drinking for solace and as a means to cope with financial and other life pressures. When I was grown, married, and had children, I developed a drinking problem of my own. My son also turned to drugs and alcohol. I got sober thirty-three years ago, and my son is now sober, too, but it was a long hard journey.

My son had blamed me for who he had become during those dark days, but I made amends to him. The wall came down between us when I told him that I would never put another expectation on him again. This freed me to be myself and focus on my life and what I was doing instead of what my son was doing. I let my son experience the consequences of his actions, which led to jail several times. My wife and I didn't fix his situation or bail him out. We let him do the time and learn from his mistakes.

My kids have a right to who they are and to their way of thinking. I have no right to impose my will on them or argue with them, but instead I seek to understand them. I love them for who they are and don't try to change them, just as I don't allow anyone to change me. We are all on journeys of our own.

If I focus on another's journey, it takes away from my own and the other person's as well. I now live in the moment.

One of my favorite memories when my children were growing up was the time we rented a home in Arrowhead during Christmas. We bought a pine tree for one dollar at a local fire department, and the money went to charity. My kids made the Nativity scene from whatever they found in the mountains, such as peanut shells. They also linked loops of paper together in a chain, which they wrapped around our tree. We had no phone or television to distract us, only radio music which we enjoyed. We worked together and had fun. My family still talks about this special time.

My greatest challenge in fatherhood, as well in life, has been learning to deal with my "negative" thoughts. I used to speak critically to myself which made matters worse. I learned that negative thinking brings negative results, so I committed to thinking positively.

Once, when my wife and I were traveling in Italy, we were confused about how to get to our hotel. Instead of blaming myself or others, my wife and I went straight to the solution. We accepted that our cab ride was going to be long and expensive. It lasted about one and a half hours, and we paid a high fair. The money was not as important as our emotional well-being. We accepted the "negative" event and focused on solving it. This gave us the peace to think clearly and enjoy the ride instead of being distressed.

I'm fortunate to have raised a son and a daughter and now to have four grandchildren. I hope that they all live happy lives, enjoying who they are. I have learned that all people are God's precious children and should be treated with dignity and respect. This includes me! Love, I found, was the key to everything, and I have finally learned to love myself.

From this place of self-love, I came to love all around me. When I wake up in the morning, negative thoughts come to my mind. I consciously get rid of them, I don't need them. Positive thoughts then fill my mind, and I do what's in front of me to do and enjoy it, including cooking and cleaning. There are times when someone might ask me how I'm doing and I resist admitting that I'm doing better than I'd like to acknowledge. I dismiss my original thought though and answer honestly. I also pass this positive stance onto others. I subscribe to the saying, "If you see someone without a smile, give them one of yours." When I see people who aren't smiling, I smile at them. They usually smile back, and I see relief and happiness in their face. One time, I smiled at someone and then noticed I was still smiling as I walked away. I felt great and realized I was living in the moment, enjoying the simple act of exchanging a smile.

I have also learned to accept the negative behavior of others. My son currently lives with my wife and me, and if his behavior is bothering me, I usually ignore it. If, however, it infringes on my wife's and my comfort, I talk to my son in a civil tone. I tell him that his behavior is not good for him, my wife, or me, and that he can either do the right thing or move out. During these conversations, I always emphasize that I love my son. I seek to follow the wisdom of the prayer of St. Francis of Assisi:

"Lord, make me an instrument of Thy peace;…
Oh Divine Master, Grant that I may not so much seek
To be consoled, as to console;
To be understood, as to understand; To be loved,
as to love…"

I have learned to enjoy who my children are now and not force them into who I "think" they should be. This process of discovery and acceptance took time. In accepting myself, others, and life, I live in the surrendered state of, "Thy will be done."

I have experienced such wonderful results from living a life of love and acceptance. I have peaceful relations with others even in stressful situations. I noticed this especially with my dad. His drinking increased as he aged, and he often had bouts of paranoia. One time he accused me of not picking him up on time. Instead of arguing back, I calmly replied, "Dad, I would not do that. I love you. I'll call you later when you're feeling better, and we'll go out to eat." This de-escalated my father's fear and anger and shifted the conversation to a positive tone. I understood that my father had a difficult life, which contributed to his alcoholism. When others were no longer there for him due to his mental and emotional decline, my acceptance of my father allowed me to be there for him until he passed away.

At home, I love my wife for who she is. I recall a time when she was watching a TV show that I considered "silly," but I kept my mouth shut instead of voicing my opinion. I saw that she was enjoying it, and I found pleasure seeing her enjoy herself. I want to be free to be myself, so I let others be free to be themselves. I am excited to say that my wife and I have been married fifty-five years as a result of practicing love and acceptance.

Love and acceptance have been the answer. They always will be.

***Today, let's give a smile of love
and acceptance to those who don't have one and
brighten our world one smile at a time.***

11

COMMITTED

"Fatherhood is a choice and a commitment.
Any man can make a child but a real father is committed to
his kids and honors his divine call of being a father."

✣

Pastor Bayless Conley

GOD IN ALL

Pastor Bayless Conley
California

J.J. – I interviewed Pastor Bayless Conley in his office at Cottonwood Church in Los Alamitos, CA, where he and his wife, Janet, serve as Senior Pastors. He has a local congregation of eight thousand and hosts a weekly television show ministering to viewers in over 200 nations.

Prior to our interview, I felt nervous about meeting a pastor of such renown. When I met him, he was wearing a Hawaiian shirt and flip-flops from just having conducted a Hawaiian funeral. He greeted me with a friendly smile and a cool bottle of water, which calmed my speeding heart and put me at ease. He ministers to millions, but that day, he ministered to me by his kindness and hospitality. I now offer his wisdom as a father to minister to your heart as well.

—

My father has always been a man of great character, keeping his word. He told me, "Son, never be quick to give someone your word, but if you give it, it's sacred." This advice has been invaluable to me because it's taught me to be a man of integrity. I'm careful about giving my word, because if I give it, I need to keep it or die trying to keep it. Many people don't see the value in this; they over-promise and under- deliver. This breeds a lack of trust, so I keep my word, which builds trust and good faith in my personal and business relationships.

My father also instilled a love of the outdoors in me. We went backpacking in the wilderness every weekend when I was a boy. He went upstream, and I went downstream, alone. We'd meet back in the evening, sit around the fire, and eat the fish we'd caught. We'd spend two to three days like this together, with just a dozen spoken words between us, but those quiet times spoke volumes. Words are a bit like coins though; you get too many in circulation, and they lose their value. My father is still not a man of many words but I felt a special connection, just being quiet with him. Those backpacking trips with my father helped shape me into the person I am today. I've learned to be content with my own company. I love people, but I don't have to be around people or need applause to make me happy.

My wife and I have two adult sons, a daughter, and two young grandsons. As I raised my kids, I wanted them to discover and walk in what God had called and created them to do. My wife and I prayed that God would show us what our children's natural gifts were. I never fashioned them in my own image or made them do what I thought they should do. I think it's a great mistake to push one's son or daughter to be a surgeon or concert violinist, etc. The question is, "What has God created this person to do?" "Train up a child in the way he should go [and in keeping with his individual gift or bent], and when he is old he will not depart from it." (Proverbs 22:6 AMP)

I wanted to help my kids find, develop, and flourish in their innate bent, whether it was being an artist, a teacher, or whatever else. I don't separate work as secular or sacred. God can give a person a sphere of influence within any profession; whatever a person is called to do, can be done unto God.

My father never pushed me into something that wasn't right for me. He loves football more than anyone I know, He even played for Bear Bryant at the University of Kentucky. He would've been delighted if I'd pursued football, but I wasn't interested in it. I loved baseball and fishing, so he took up fishing, which he'd never done, and attended all my baseball games. I'm so grateful that he let me be me. We all have a unique calling, but a person can have everything in life: financial success, applause from others, live in the nicest place; but if he or she doesn't have a relationship with God, it's empty. That was the number one thing which I taught my kids: have a relationship with God.

As a father, the first part of my role is to love my kids unconditionally. If they misbehaved, my wife and I disciplined them and assured them that we still loved them. We were patient parents. We talked a great deal about consequences, but if our children insisted on repeating a behavior, we spanked them. The Bible says, "Foolishness is bound into the heart of a child, but the rod of correction shall drive it far from him." (Proverbs 22:15)

I believe spending time with your kids is a top priority. As a father, it's been challenging to balance the busyness of ministry with time for my family. My priorities are my relationship with God, my wife, kids, and then the church. It's been a juggling act, and sometimes I've felt like I was spinning plates. One time, just before our house was to be tented for termites, I took one of my boys fishing. I'd forgotten to get the fishing poles out of the garage, so when I went back to get them, I told the exterminator that I was taking my boy fishing. He was a big, burly guy who said, "That must be nice," in a cynical tone. I replied, "Taking my boy fishing is not a luxury, it's a necessity."

He teared up and said, "You're right. I missed my kids growing up. I was never there for them. I was always busy with the job. You're doing the right thing. Go enjoy the time with your boy."

Some people say they give their kids quality time, but I think quality comes out of quantity. I'd tell a new father to give his kids as much time as he can, and he'll get some quality within that.

Sticking to these core values, however, has made decision-making easier though. If the decision would hurt my family, the answer was, "No." We have a worldwide television ministry with offices in seven nations. When I started on TV, I drove one to two nights a week to a studio to record the show. I remember my eldest son being at the door, hanging onto me, and saying, "Dad, I want you. Don't go." Then he'd cry. I'd drive down the street, park, and put my head on the steering wheel and sob. I spoke with our church leadership, and we invested in the equipment to bring the studio in-house. Since I didn't go away those evenings anymore, by the time my oldest son reached eighteen, I'd been able to spend one more entire year of evenings with him. Moving the studio to the church had God's blessing and direction, but my motivation was to spend time with my son.

I believe the best way to teach is by example. I showed my kids my love for their mother and was always affectionate with her. Oh, they've seen us fight, too, and they've seen us make up. They know we're committed to each other and that divorce has never been in our vocabulary. We have differences, but we work through them. We have been married thirty-two years. Hopefully, my kids will emulate the same commitment when all of them are married.

Fatherhood is a choice and a commitment. Any man can make a child, but a real father is committed to his kids and honors his divine call of being a father. There isn't just one way to be a father though. God uses my wiring and personality, and I'm a dad that way. Another dad might be more artsy or musical than me. God is in that father and in his personality just as much as he's in me. There's a myriad of different kinds of dads and ways to be a father. It all has to do with howGod has wired the man. A man shouldn't feel condemned or compare himself to another dad's fathering style. God can bless him just as much, and his kids can grow up to be awesome people in a different environment. The key is to keep God in the center of his parenting.

Now that my kids are grown, my role has shifted in their lives. I don't watch over them as when they were young, but I'm there for them and have regular contact with them. We have family night every Tuesday at my home. My kids, parents, and grandkids all come. I cook, and we hang around together. The grandkids and I fish, wrestle, play games, and shoot at each other with dart guns. It's mayhem, and it's wonderful!

I've now entered a new season in my life which has greatly impacted my family and work at the church. In January 2014, I was severely injured in a boating accident near Catalina. My friends and I planned to free dive for lobster, but we hit a small outcropping of rocks on a moonless night. I was airlifted to the mainland in time. Fifteen minutes later and I wouldn't have survived. I spent many weeks in ICU in the hospital and then recuperated for several months at home. My throat was crushed, so I couldn't swallow and was fed by a feeding tube. My speech was so slurred that people couldn't understand me. My family prayed and stood by me throughout. My wife was an absolute champion. It was scary for my kids to face the reality that they might lose their dad. All my doctors thought I'd die. If I did live, they didn't know if I'd ever function properly because of the bleeding on my brain, if I'd be incapacitated physically and mentally, or if my days of ministry were over. If I did recover, it might take year and a half before I could speak well enough to even preach again.

It's been seven months since the accident, and I'm preaching again! The experience made me rethink my priorities. I'll still preach, but I'll share the load more with other church leaders. The church grew in unity, influence, and numerically while I was gone because these leaders stepped up to help.

My recovery has reinforced the fact that God often restores us in process. In church, we often preach about the events, the sudden things God does. We applaud those, but much of what God does is via process. The bleeding on my brain stopped on its own, but my speech is being restored slowly. I had to learn to talk again and put my tongue in different places for some sounds. My speech gets better every day. I've learned to trust God in the midst of the process, whether it's a process of physical recovery, financial recovery, or any type of growth or healing. People get discouraged when things take longer than they want. I rejoice while the process is happening and don't just celebrate the event.

GOD IN ALL

God's wisdom turned this near tragedy into a blessing. My relationships with God and my family deepened, and our church grew stronger. God has blessed me with many joys, and my greatest joy as a father is seeing my kids love God, be honest human beings and have integrity. To quote the third Epistle of John, "I have no greater joy than to hear that my children are walking in the truth." (3 John 1:4 NIV)

Today, let's rejoice and trust in God for whatever process or season of life we're in.

TEEN DAD TO TRANSFORMED LIFE

Joe Chavez
California

I was eighteen years old when my girlfriend told me I was going to be a dad. I was so nervous, I was sick to my stomach! My girlfriend was so stressed, she cried herself to sleep. This couldn't have happened at a worse time. I had just been released on bail and was facing fifteen years in jail with three counts of assault with a deadly weapon, home invasion, robbery, and breaking and entering. I was into drugs at the time and had gone with a group of guys to retaliate the beating of one of our friends. I did not participate in the fight, but I damaged some property. Six police officers showed up in the college class I was attending and took me to jail.

A short time before this incident, I started going to the youth group at my church and made the decision to always tell the truth. When the police officers asked if I had done the crime, I said, "Yes." I didn't know it then, but that day was the end of my old life; and restoration and a wonderful life lay ahead of me. Most of my family doubted I could be a good father, and my mother could only cry when she heard the news. I felt sad about their lack of faith in me, but I knew that my irresponsible path gave them no confidence. My grandmother was the only one happy for us. She told us to trust God and go with it, which is what I planned to do. I was rebellious, and I took it as a challenge to become a husband and father.

I finally felt like my life was my own, and I could make decisions without needing others' approval. I served my time in jail, blaming everybody else for my problems: my family, friends, and anyone else I could think of. I finally realized it was my fault that I was in the mess I was in, and it was up to me to rely on God to change. I'm glad I finally realized this. Several of my friends who were in the crime with me did not take responsibility and still have trouble with the law today. I am free from such worries!

After three months in jail, I was released on good behavior. The baby was yet to be born, and the shock of real life as an adult hit me hard. My girlfriend and I got married and lived with my family at first. So many people gave us advice, but I was so very young, and every day was a struggle in the grown-up world. I had never worked, and I looked tirelessly online for jobs. I finally got a job at Taco Bell, but I had also lost my license due to a DUI, so I either rode my bike or ran the couple of miles to work. I was also attending school full-time. I was running on pure adrenaline, doing whatever I could to earn money to support my wife and soon-to-be born baby.

At nineteen years old I became a father. I wished that I had a father around to guide me. My parents were both sixteen years old when I was born and never married. My dad left town right away and I've only seen him seven times in my life, and the last time when I was thirteen years old. I was raised by my maternal grandparents, so my grandfather was dad to me. In fourth grade, I moved back in with my mom. It was hard to be the man of the house at ten years old. I missed the guidance of having a strong male figure at home. I was my own final authority and wanted someone to tell me right from wrong and to give me wisdom in the moment. When I became a father, I wondered, "How could my father have left me? I love my son so much!"

So here I was, a new dad and husband, living at home with my mom and grandparents. My wife and I tried to be as independent as possible, so we paid rent and bought our own groceries. It was good training before we moved out on our own. I had always loved art and was voted the most artistic of my senior class. I had no outlet for my angst and desire to create, so I had expressed myself in graffiti. I knew this had been wrong and had damaged property. I was now committed to living a sober, godly life, and decided to volunteer to help in the art department at my church. In volunteering for the art department, I felt I could use my artistic talents for a good, honorable purpose.

I met the art director, and he became a mentor who helped me grow. He told me that God loves and accepts me just as I am. I felt accepted by him and encouraged that art was the right direction for my life. His acceptance of me reflected God's acceptance of me. I had felt shame about my past, but he taught me that my past was valuable and that I have learned many lessons at a young age which I could pass on to others.

Under this new mentor, I fell in love with graphic design work. Could people really make a living doing this? He assured me that this was possible. I was so excited that I downloaded a free trial of Adobe Creative Suite and taught myself some programs. I saw an ad for a job at a chiropractor's office as a graphic designer, so I drove there the next day with designs I had done with my free download and prayed to God to give me the right words to speak.

It was a miracle that my car sputtered and died just as I pulled in to the parking space of the doctor's office, because it had been slowly dying all the way to the interview. I told God, "I either get this job, or I'm done." I showed the chiropractor my designs, and he hired me! It was $10 dollars an hour, so I kept my job at Taco Bell. I was now working two jobs, going to school full-time, being a husband, and raising my baby. All these responsibilities were rough on a young father like me, but I was determined to give it my all.

One day, the art director called and offered me a part-time job as a graphic designer at the church. Of course, I accepted! I quit my two jobs and school and focused on my design work at the church. This act of faith paid off; I was soon offered a full-time position at the church with benefits.

Today, at age twenty-three, my life is completely different than when I first got the terrifying news that I was going to be a dad. My son is now four years old, and I'm committed to being present with him. I understand why some guys leave. When it gets really hard, I've wanted to run away. I don't because I love my wife and son and am determined to be there for them. I will never leave.

This experience led me to create a blog called, Empowering Young Families, to help young families start smart.[6] It's the first online platform dedicated to helping young families thrive. Once a week, I post practical information to help families live independently and provide tools for adulthood. I cover topics such as budgeting, gratitude, and the wisdom of taking one thing at a time.

When I felt overwhelmed in my life, I wanted to change everything at once. I wanted to buy my son a sled full of toys at Christmas, but instead, I needed to get him a few items at Dollar Tree. I now live more prosperously and can be more generous with my family, but the increases have come slowly over time. I tell families that learning to manage money is more im-

---

[6] www.empoweringyoungfamilies.com

portant than making money. I've also written a book of tips for young people to help them increase their success in life.

One of the most helpful things for me as a father and busy professional is my morning routine. I get up at 5 a.m. and then have three fifteen-minute blocks, where I exercise, read the Bible, and plan my day before the household is awake. I do this every morning, seven days a week. I cook breakfast for my family, so that when they get up, we can enjoy it together in peace. This routine decreases my stress and increases my ability to be present with my family and for my work. It gives me an edge for my day. In my book and blog, I encourage young family members to establish a morning routine to gain some structure and spiritual guidance for their days.

My wife and I are now expecting our second child. This time, I am excited instead of filled with apprehension. I'm taking birthing classes with my wife and am completely involved in the process. I want to experience every drop of this. When I was in the delivery room for our first baby, I fainted! Since I never give up though, I will be in the delivery room for our second child coaching my wife through an all- natural birth.

I have so much joy in being a father. I love hearing my son's voice; it's so sweet and tender. It's such a joy to pick him up, hold him like a plane, and swirl him around as he calls out, "Daddy, I'm flying!" We have fun riding skateboards, playing catch and tag. Most nights we have story time together. Right now his favorite book is *All by Myself* by Mercer Mayer. The main character tries to do everything by himself but still needs a lot of help. This is my son. He's more independent than when he was a baby, but he realizes that he still needs his parents. I'm grateful that he knows he has parents who he can count on. Growing up without a father, I did not have such grace.

I teach my son to never give up. I've told him this so many times, that we have videos of him saying, "I will never give up!" My son loves puzzles, and sometimes he wants to quit when he can't find a piece. I tell him to persist, and I walk him through the process of finding the missing piece. I ask him questions, such as, "When did you last have it? Where did you last see it?" He has lost numerous pieces, and through this question-and-answer process, he has found every one. If the time comes when he doesn't find a piece, I will still praise him for having looked. It's more important that he gives it his all instead of not trying.

Although I teach my son to give his all to everything, I also tell him to trust God for everything he doesn't have. I've learned that even when I gave it my all, it was not enough. I still needed God. When I'm open to God's power and guidance though, miracles happen. On my own, I ended up in jail. With God, I have a beautiful wife and son, a job that I love being of service and expressing my art, and new opportunities to contribute to young families through my blog.

My son will never know all that I have done for him out of love. Likewise, I will never know how much God has done for me. I know that God loves me and that I love my son. Just as I help guide my son find the missing piece in his puzzles, God helped me find the missing piece within me–love and acceptance, first from God and now for myself and others. Being a father is a part of this package of love. If my son is ever asked about me, I hope that he'll answer, "My dad is full of grace." God granted me grace when he led me out of a life of drugs, drinking, and destruction to a new life as a dedicated father, husband, and worker.

I'm so grateful that I didn't check out of life when the going got rough as a young dad. I broke through the fear in those hard times. When my son says, "Daddy, I love you," I know that all the hours I spent reflecting on life while in jail, taking drive-through orders at Taco Bell, and learning graphic design, have been worth it. My journey to this love started by being a teen dad. I'm so fortunate to be a father. It is my highest privilege. I don't have to be a dad; I get to be a dad!

Today, let's give our all to everything we undertake and be grateful for the many anonymous graces we have received in our lives.

"POST THE SCORE"

Jerry Cozby
Oklahoma

J.J. – Jerry Cozby was a head club golf professional for forty-one years and earned numerous awards, such as being the 1985 PGA Professional of the Year and a 2005 Inductee to the PGA Golf Professional Hall Of Fame. He was also Golfweek's Father of the Year for 2012. When we spoke on the phone for the interview, other than mentioning winning one tournament, he never shared about any of his accolades. Humbly, he was a husband and father first, golfer second.

—

During the oil boom, many families moved to Texas for a new start in life. My mother and father had worked for an oil company there, and in 1941, I was born and spent my growing years in West Texas. My father taught me good old-fashioned values such as working hard, doing what you say you're going to do, and treating people right. He taught me to do the right thing and always to give my all in whatever I did in life.

I later married, and my wife and I have three sons, now adults; and five grandchildren. I love being around my grandkids and watching them grow. I also love watching my sons raise their kids and be leaders for them.

I pursued my love of golf and ended up working as a club golf professional at the Hillcrest Country Club in Bartlesville, Oklahoma, six days a week and on holidays. Fortunately, since

I was the head professional, I was able to maintain my job responsibilities and keep my family number one. My sons were into athletics, and whenever I could attend my sons' functions, I was there. If I couldn't go, my wife was there. We worked together to always support our sons. My kids also came to the club, and we golfed together. I always believed in the value of athletics to make our bodies healthy.

As a club professional, I competed with other club professionals. All three of my sons excelled in golf as well and were successful and accomplished players for the University of Oklahoma golf team. When they started traveling to tournaments, I knew that I could not do my job, play in my own tournaments, and attend my sons' tournaments. When my sons were in college, I stopped competing so that I could continue to do my work at the club and travel to support my sons. I also told my sons that after they won, they didn't need to brag about it; if they were really good, others already knew it. I simply said, "Post the score; don't worry about anything else."

My sons' participation in golf has brought us family treasures. My eldest son, Cary, had great success when he wore a black cap for his tournaments. He then passed it onto my middle son, Craig, and he later passed it onto my youngest son, Chance. The cap was originally black and said, "Just Do It–Sooners" on the front. After being worn for many years, the hat faded into khaki from the sweat and weather on the golf course. In 1999, my sons put the cap in a glass case and gave it to my wife and me as a present. The front of the case lists their golf accomplishments and says:

"POST THE SCORE"

To Mom and Dad:

11 "O" Letters
6 First-Team All-Big 8 Awards (now the Big 12)
2 All-American Awards
1 Big 8 Newcomer of the Year Award
1 NCAA Team Championship
1 Big 8 Team Championship
3 "O" Rings
1 Cap

Merry Christmas!
Cary, Craig and Chance

    My family's involvement in golf has also united us closer. Cary is now forty-six years old, and when he was nine, I played in a section golf tournament, which had players in it from two and a half states. I won the tournament and played thirty-six holes a day for three days straight. Cary asked to join me, and he rode with me in the cart for the entire tournament. He is now a club golf professional, and although he never said anything, perhaps that special ride we shared in the golf cart and the bonding we experienced influenced him to later become a golf professional. The *Tulsa World Newspaper* also wrote an article about the closeness Cary and I shared as he accompanied me in the tournament.

    The love is so deep of being a father, that words can't describe it. When I was young and raising my family, I took care of things as they arose. Now that I am seventy-three, I look back and wonder, how did I do it? How did I get them educated and raise them to be adults? If I had known everything that I was going to go through as a dad, I would've been scared. I was never scared though, because I "gave it my all," just like my father taught me. I also passed this ethic onto my sons and told them to give one hundred ten percent; one hundred percent was not enough. I said, "Whatever you decide to do, be excellent at it; the world's full of average people." They have all lived this guidance and now enjoy happy family lives and professional success. Cary is a golf pro at Southern Hills Country Club, which is one of the top twenty clubs in the country. My other two sons have top sales and vice president positions with one of the leading golf companies in the world. My father's guidance to give life my all has led me to the retirement stage in life where I can continue to give my all to my wife, sons, and grandchildren. A hole-in-one makes the golfer in me smile, but my family and the love we share makes me smile most of all.

Today, let's "give life our all" in everything we do and simply, "post the score" and not worry about all the rest.

J.J. – Jerry called me later in the day after reflecting upon my interview questions and added more to his responses. His wife, Karole, also contributed to the conversation, and I was touched by their commitment to share fathers' wisdom to help and inspire others. Jerry had so much joy in his voice as he spoke about his love for his family, that although I could not see him, since he was a couple thousand miles away, he sounded like he was smiling; that left me with a smile, too.

A FATHER TO COUNT ON

Joe Jimenez
California

Growing up in a single parent household where my father participated very little in my life has made me a committed father. From this experience, I have an unsaid promise to my two sons, eight months and five years old, to always be there for them and honor my responsibilities as a father. I carry this over to my job as well. As an Associate Executive Director for the YMCA, I promote character values such as respect, honesty, caring, and responsibility. These values are not just important to me professionally but are foremost in my family as well.

As part of my commitment to being there for my kids, I am attentive to keeping a work/life balance. When I'm home, I dedicate my time and energy to my wife and children. We have fun walking, playing sports, and going to the park. I enjoy learning about my sons, who they are and what they like to do, and I nurture those interests in them. My sons love Legos, so I play Legos with them. My kids are great at letting me know when I get out of balance because they'll want more attention from me. For instance, my eldest son might purposely spill milk. I then realize I need to adjust my schedule in order to give my boys more attention.

I teach my five-year-old son to be respectful by being polite and saying "please" and "thank you" in and outside of our home. Even if he's at his grandparents' house, he still needs to ask politely for something to drink. I have been teaching my eldest son to be honest. He's been exaggerating when he tells stories, so I encourage him to share more accurately.

When my wife was pregnant with our second child, we told my eldest son what was happening so that he'd know what to expect when he became a brother. He is now a kind, caring big brother and loves to share his toys with his baby brother.

I want my sons to be responsible whether they are at home, in school, or in our community. At home, my oldest son helps with chores and keeps his room clean. He does his homework at set times in order to be a responsible student. I also talk to him about the importance of giving to help others, to be socially responsible. I tell him that if he has saved some money, some can be for him, and some can be given to others. One time, when his grandmother offered to give him some money, he told her to keep it to buy herself a coffee. I felt so proud of him for being kind to his grandmother and not just thinking of himself.

As a father, I'll always treasure my sons' awesome milestones, such as when my eldest son began to talk, first counted to ten in English and Spanish, and took his first steps. Recently, he cried his first few days of kindergarten. Shortly after that, I told him that I was starting a new job at the YMCA, and he said, "Everything is going to be okay. Don't cry. You'll be able to come home afterwards." He was supporting me just as my wife and I had supported him through his first anxious days of kindergarten. He learned that he could go to school, be independent, and then come home and be with his family again. He had grown through the big step of starting school and could then assure me that I would be okay, too.

I have cherished every moment with my kids. I bring my son to school, and during the ride, we share about the day ahead, his school and what he's learning. I enjoy our family walks because we can focus on family, talk and listen to one another. In all of my parenting, my wife and I work as a team to ensure that we are encouraging our kids to be the best people possible.

My business card for the YMCA says, "Count on Us." This motto is my driving force at work and with my family. If I tell my eldest son that I'll pick him up from school or that I'll take him to buy Legos over the weekend, I keep my word. It's my unsaid promise in action–my sons can count on me.

__Today, let's be people that others can count on and fulfill all of our commitments and responsibilities.__

THE IMPORTANCE OF FIDELITY

Drue Boles
California

Although my father and I only spoke at superficial levels, not sharing emotions or talking about spirituality when I was growing up, he modeled fidelity to me. My parents were married sixty years, and this taught me that marriage was sacred. He was not an emotional man; he felt that men should not cry, but rather feel ashamed if they did. However, that did not deter me from expressing my emotions with my son and daughter, who are now adults. I wanted to model being a male who shares his feelings, speaks on a real level, and is an encourager, supporter, and disciplinarian for his kids. I'm a devoted Christian and desired to demonstrate a Christian life to them. I am an Associate Pastor, and I wanted my kids to see that I am a "real" person and not an "elevated" clergyman. I like to have fun, and I enjoyed taking my son to Dodger games and my kids to Disneyland when they grew up.

When my kids entered their teenage years, our lives were turned upside down. My wife had an affair with an elder at the church where I worked. My wife then left me and married the other man. I felt devastated. The infidelity also impacted the church where I served. This event was a crisis of faith for me.

As a Christian, I tended to deny reality and live in "La La Land." This event catapulted me into reality. Was what I told people about God's faithfulness for fifteen years in pastoral counseling real or not? My challenge was how to cope when what's not supposed to happen, happens to you. I sought out people I thought were safe to talk to and who would give me wise advice. A friend who'd experienced a similar situation told me to not talk about my ex-wife with my kids and never to speak against her with them. He cautioned me to answer graciously and honestly when my kids asked me a question about their mother.

At just eleven and thirtreen years old, my kids were now a part of a broken home. I felt the crushing blow of divorce, and I worked hard to provide a sense of normalcy for them. I sought to be a person of integrity whom my children could count on during this painful time. I set aside lunch after church on Sundays to talk with them about their feelings. My daughter feared that she might be unfaithful one day since her mother had been. I assured her that just because her mother chose that path, she did not need to repeat the cycle and could be faithful. My son had friends who cheated on their girlfriends and said he didn't know how they could do that. He was committed to being faithful to his girlfriend. He also feared marriage, and I told him that all relationships are a risk and that each person must decide whether it's worth the risk or not. These talks helped me, too, to process the good that I could find out of all this.

As I worked through my emotions, my faith was strengthened, and I learned that God is faithful and keeps His word to guide, comfort, and strengthen those in need. God's grace is sufficient. When everything that I held to be most dear was taken away, I still had hope and peace in Jesus. God's people comforted and assured me that God was near and holding onto me and my burden.

I also kept myself busy, possibly too busy, to cope with the situation. I ran on adrenaline, doing activities such as laundry and packing my kids' lunches at 1:00 a.m. I also saw a counselor who helped me learn to get angry. My ex-wife said she was sorry, but the knife still went into my heart. I set boundaries with her as an act of self-care. She would often call and talk to me for hours. I learned to not be her counselor and said that it wasn't healthy for us to be friends because it was too phony. I felt that she'd broken the next most important covenant in life after the covenant one has with God.

I also learned that forgiveness doesn't mean forgetting nor does it change reality. It comes gradually as we let go of bitterness and move on freely with our life. Forgiveness has different levels, and as I'd get through one thing, another would come. All of the firsts as a single parent were difficult, such as the first birthday and Christmas. My emotions got raw again, and I alternated between feeling angry and sad. Everything was forever different. The divorce was like a death, but harder, since I still had to deal with my ex-wife.

When I was still healing from my marriage, I met the woman who later became my wife. I was ready to marry her after four months, but she said it was too soon. We waited three years, and my wife and I now enjoy a long-term marriage of joy, faithfulness, honesty, and intimacy.

I was granted full legal custody of my children. My wife, perhaps out of guilt, signed everything over to me. I was advised to move quickly with the divorce terms, and I did. I wanted my kids to see a healthy marriage and didn't want them to see their dad living as a victim waiting for their mother to return after the tryst. I also wanted them to see me being strong in Christ and not emotionally destroyed by someone else.

As a father, I pass on this: our greatest commitment is to God and building a relationship with Jesus. I also teach my kids to be people of integrity, for having a good reputation cannot be replaced. I emphasize to my kids and others to protect the fidelity of their marriage, and that no person is worth letting their soul be trampled upon. I've grown through the pain and lessons of infidelity and divorce and now gladly share the wisdom I've gained to help those in my midst.

Today, let's live the wise path of fidelity and integrity in all of our relationships and deeds.

12

TOLERANCE

"There is no reason to hate one another;
we are created equally...There are no races,
only one race–the human race."

✜

Bernard Savone

COURAGE AND INSPIRATION

Steve Monroney
Colorado

Every family has had times when they face hurdles and challenges of various kinds. As a runner, I understand this quite well. In 2013, I ran the Boston Marathon and finished the race just before the bomb went off. When I had finally made the heartfelt decision to acknowledge to my family that I was gay, it was as if a bomb had gone off emotionally. My children had to work through the tangle of feelings, and it was a painful time for all of us. This was such unfamiliar territory to walk in at the time, and I am sure they felt alone, but I am proud they were able to accept my lifestyle and be at peace with what I knew was the right path for me.

As an accomplished track athlete, it has become a part of living my truth to participate every four years in the Gay Games, which are held around the world. In 2004, in Montréal, I ran the 800 meter, 1500 meter, 4 kilometer and half marathon in one week. I placed fourth in the first three events and won the silver medal in the half marathon. In 2010, in Cologne, Germany, I won gold medals in the 4 x 100, 4 x 200 and 4 x 400 meter relays. Due to my success, a journalist wanted to write an article about me. At the time, I had not been very public about being gay, so to be considerate of my children, I asked them if it'd be okay to have the article published. Both my children agreed to the publication. The article made the front page of the Sports Section in *The Greeley Tribune*. My daughter was glad that the article was published, because her father's being gay was no longer a secret. The truth was out, which was a great relief. My kids were also proud of me for coming out and for my athletic prowess.

My daughter, who is now twenty-three years old, lives with her fiancé, and my nineteen year old son still lives at home with me. Both of my kids are highly intelligent, and I hope that they harness their intelligence and energy and contribute something of value to the world. I never want my kids to give up on reaching their goals. My daughter is pursuing a degree in Neuropsychology, and I encourage her to be persistent and keep at it. As her father, I am also her coach, cheering her on. I've showed both my kids how to reach smaller goals as they work toward long-term ones. I want them both to live a balanced life of work and play.

If one-third of my role as a father is a coach, I would have to say the other two-thirds would be as a friend and mentor. As their friend, I am there for them when they need someone to talk to whom they trust. I don't just say this, I model being a trusted friend to them whenever I can. As their mentor, my goal is to guide them and help them to sort things out, like the direction they want to go in life, hopefully without controlling them! It is a challenging job of juggling these hats at times, but my kids are worth it.

My father taught me to treat people well and to give them the benefit of the doubt whenever possible. I teach my kids the same thing, to respect people from various backgrounds and cultures. My father was a salesman and had the talent and personality to woo people by listening to them and interacting with them in a positive way. I gained strong people skills from him, which have been an asset for me, especially on the job where I work as a project manager. I wanted my children to understand this in a tangible way, so I traveled with them abroad to expose them to other cultures at a young age. Sometimes the best teacher is experience.

Being a gay father makes no difference to my parenting. My family is just like a family with heterosexual parents. I have the same joys of seeing my children be happy. We go shopping, spend time together, go on vacations, etc. Fatherhood is filled with challenges; in fact, it's probably the hardest thing one will ever do, but the most rewarding. Being a father changes a person. We have a greater depth of compassion for people and appreciation for things in life other than work. Men can develop these qualities without having children, but being a father forces one to foster them.

I became a father in my twenties, and it was difficult because I didn't have much money then. If I did it over, I would wait a little longer. I spent a lot of time working to provide food, clothes, housing, and other necessities for my family. I wanted to spend more time with them, but the necessity of work limited that. Now that I'm older and have had more professional success and financial prosperity, I have time to spend with my kids, but they're busy with their adult lives and don't have as much time to spend with me. I enjoy my children. I love being mentor and coach to them and have reaped great rewards.

J.J. – To live one's truth takes tremendous courage and strength of character. Steve Monroney models a man who lives his truth and inspires others to do the same.

Today, let's live with courage and be who we are in all areas of our lives.

WWII JAPANESE-AMERICAN WAR RELOCATION CENTER SURVIVOR

James Tanaka
California

J.J. – I interviewed James Tanaka at the Japanese American National Museum in Los Angeles, CA where he serves as a tour and gallery docent.

—

It was September of 1942 when my family took the long train ride to Minidoka, Idaho. Pearl Harbor, Hawaii, had just been bombed the previous December, leading the United States into war with Japan. Since my family and I were Japanese-Americans, the United States Government had concerns about the loyalty of the 110,000 people of Japanese descent, two thirds of whom were United States citizens, and imprisoned us during the war. The propaganda of the time told Japanese-Americans that they were being patriotic by going to camp. Who were we to refuse to be called patriotic?

I was eight years old and this was my first train ride, so in my innocence, I thought it was an adventure. The Minidoka Camp had tar paper-covered barracks, coal-burning stoves, and no running water, interior walls or insulation. Our room had three cots with straw mattresses. The restrooms had ten toilets, five facing one way and five the other. Barbed wires, guard towers, and armed guards provided security for the 950- acre site where nearly 9,000 of us were held.[7] All had made similar jour-

[7]http://www.bookmice.net/darkchilde/japan/camp.html

neys with little more than what they could carry. I remember a little red scooter my parents had bought for me to strengthen my leg after being hurt in a pedestrian car accident. I was forced to give it away because I could not take it with me. Many Japanese-Americans lost personal property which they were prevented from taking with them.

My family coped with the incarceration through the Japanese philosophy, "What will be, will be." We made the best of it by earning an income at the Farm Labor Camp. We all worked at harvesting the sugar beets that grew on the farm. We also pulled weeds and thinned out beets. I later started school in the labor camp, attended one week, and then was off a couple weeks to harvest potatoes. I earned ten cents for each sack I managed to fill.

Life was even harder after the war. We had no place to go. Then in 1948, my mother passed away at age forty from an illness she'd contracted on the Farm Labor Camp. In our most desperate moments, we lived off chickens' feet and potatoes. We eventually wound up in Los Angeles.

I learned the value of accomplishment and persistence through watching my father's hard work and endurance during and after the war. He taught me to follow the rules, which I did in camp and in my family. I realized it was my camp experience that had made me such a "stickler for rules." When I was old enough, I joined the military and then went to college through the G.I. Bill. I found a career as a high school teacher and taught science for thirty-nine years before retiring. I started a family of my own which included two wonderful boys.

I used to think that my life was a rocky road, but I now believe it's more like a ribbon; it can be smooth, ruffled, or split. These ribbons twist and turn in a colorful Maypole of Life, where all kinds of ribbons meet and intersect. My rocky road of incarceration in World War II has given me valuable, meaningful lessons. I pass on what I have learned to my two sons, who are now adults. I want them to respect others, to be responsible citizens, and to avoid such traps as drugs or alcohol. I hug my kids and hold them close, unlike my father who struggled to be physically affectionate.

I currently volunteer at the Japanese American National Museum to educate the public about the Japanese-American incarceration in World War II and the prejudice that occurred during the time. There was no doubt internment was a violation of our constitutional rights and never should have happened. After the war, little evidence was ever found of the Japanese-Americans' disloyalty to the U.S. A big step in the healing process happened on February 24, 1983, when a Congressional Commission issued a report entitled "Personal Justice Denied," condemning the incarceration as "unjust and motivated by racism rather than real military necessity."[8]

Finally in 1988, a big step in the healing process occurred when President Reagan signed legislation apologizing for the imprisonment on behalf of the U.S. Government and said the actions were based on "race prejudice, war hysteria, and a lack of political leadership."[9]

I hope that my story, the resilience of my fellow detainees, and my work in helping others to be educated about what happened, might prevent such atrocities from ever recurring. I am glad my sons did not have to go through the same rocky road I did. My desire is that they can still gain the understanding, the strength to tell my story long after I am gone.

---

[8] http://encyclopedia.densho.org/Civil_Liberties_Act_of_1988/
[9] www.nytimes.com/1992/07/05/books/l-a-failure-of-leadership-489592.html

Today, let's weave the smooth, ruffled and split ribbons of our lives into resilience, respect and responsible choices for ourselves and our children.

HARD WORK AND PERSISTENCE BRING LIBERTY

Tomas Kovar
Slovakia/Chile/United States

J.J. – I interviewed Tomas Kovar at the Los Angeles Museum of the Holocaust where he first spoke to students and other museum visitors about his experiences in the Holocaust. I then spoke privately with Tomas and his wife, Rita.

—

I grew up in Zabokreky nad Nitrou, Slovakia, where my father managed a wheat, tobacco, vinegar, and alcohol farm for a wealthy Jewish owner. When World War II began, the owner was sent to a concentration camp. The Slovakian president's secretary then took over the farm and asked my father to run it, and in return, he would protect us. My father had always been a hard worker, and thanks to the excellent job he had done, we were not sent to the camps. We also wore a small yellow star on our clothes to identify us as protected Jews compared to the unprotected Jews who wore a large yellow star, most of whom were sent to the camps.

We lived on the farm until the last six months of the war, when Germany occupied Slovakia. When the Secretary said that he could no longer protect us, my father decided to follow the Partisans, the Slovakian Resistance, to the mountains above the village. I rode on our horse-drawn, four- wheel carriage, which my father had loaded with food and supplies. The Partisans gave up, but we continued and lived in the mountains one week. Then some men from the village of Ponicka Huta came up to the mountains looking for plunder but instead found a group of Jews, including us. My father approached one of them, Mr. Alexander Kur, and offered to pay him if he would hide us. He agreed, so my father, mother and I hid in his home for the next six months. Fortunately, my father had wisely saved his money and could now provide for our safety. The Kur family took a great risk in hiding us, because if the Germans caught them, they would kill them and us as well. Mr. and Mrs. Kur's names are listed as Righteous Among the Nations on a memorial wall at the Museum of the Holocaust in Jerusalem.

I was eight years old when we went into hiding. Whenever Germans came through the village looking for Jews to take to the camps, we hid in special places. If we only had short notice, we hid in the four and a half foot by four and a half foot cellar, which was beneath a rug in the living room. The Kur family had an armoire in front of a wall with a storage room behind it. Mr. Kur took out the back panel and filled it with clothes so that it looked normal. If we had more time to hide, we climbed through the armoire and hid in the storage room. If we had still more time, we ran to the forest beyond the village for the greatest safety. Since I was a child, I had no idea that our lives hung by a thread. To me, hiding and hearing bombs were normal, for most of my life had been lived during the war.

Toward the end of the war, Germans came through Slovakian villages searching for men to fight since so many of their soldiers had been killed. All the men in the village, Jews and non-Jews, took to hiding in the forest. They made a bunker out of a large hole covered with a board and leaves. During this time, Germans came looking for Jews. My mother and I thought we had enough time to go to the forest, so I ran right away. My mother went to get a jacket, but the Germans came too quickly, and she was forced to hide in the cellar. I felt terrified being alone in the forest. I got lost and didn't know my way back. I had no idea if my mother was alive, and she was panicked not knowing if I was alive. My father taught me to be brave and persistent though, so I kept walking. Eventually, I saw a man chopping wood, and he showed me the way back to the village. When I made it back home, my mother and I were so happy and relieved to learn that we were both alive!

Then one night, some Russian soldiers knocked on the door and asked where the German trenches were because they wanted to attack them and liberate us. My mother and several women from the village took them to the bunker where the men were hiding, and my father volunteered to go to their general and tell him where the trenches were located. The next night, the Russians defeated the Germans in the trenches. Soldiers came knocking on doors to tell us all that the village was liberated. My father was never listed in the village's history as the man who helped liberate it. One of my sons has planned to write a letter to the city government to request that he be included in their village history to honor his contribution.

After the war, we returned to our home village, and my father managed the farm as before. However, on September 24, 1945, persecution broke out against Jews in an anti-Jewish riot (pogrom) in Topoľčany. A Jewish doctor, who had returned from Auschwitz, was giving smallpox vaccines to Christian children and was accused of injecting them with poison. Rumors spread, and soon a group of Slovaks attacked the doctor and other Jews. My father hurriedly applied for a visa to the United States but was denied since the quota for immigrants was met. Instead, we boarded a ship for Chile, where my father had a cousin. When we arrived in BuenosAires in 1947, President Peron would not let us off the ship for three days until the train came to take us to Chile. Many Nazis went to Argentina after the war, and he was getting money from them.

In Chile, my father rented a farm and worked just as hard as usual. I went to school and helped on the farm. The farm workers, however, took advantage of him and complained to the labor board about him. Finally, the inspector came and saw that my father was an honorable man who worked extremely hard and then left him alone. Once again, my father's hard work paid off, and we lived in peace. My father never had it easy working the land. He was not appreciated or paid much. He was a strong family man though and did whatever he could to support my mother and me so that we could live better lives.

I later married in Chile, and in 1966, we moved to the United States. I ran Hallmark stores, and my three children helped us. Family is most important to me, as it was to my father. Although I spent much time working, I also enjoyed playing soccer with my kids and going on our annual vacations. I was always an involved and dedicated father and insisted that we share our family meals together. During this time, we discussed our problems and issues openly. My wife and I never disagreed in front of our children and always respected one another's decisions. As a father, I sought to guide my children and hoped that they would follow in the path which I felt was best. I'm grateful that I had success in that, for whatever my wife and I planted, grew healthy. I am proud of who my children are, and it's fun to brag about them.

My father's name was Ernest, and his name fit him because he always worked in earnest and taught me to do the same. I have been a hard, serious worker all my life. I am now retired, but I continue to work as a Spanish interpreter for orthopedic doctors. I also passed on the value of hard work to my children, and they are all successful in their professions.

In retirement, I also share about the Holocaust by speaking in schools and at the Los Angeles Museum of the Holocaust. I tell people that the Holocaust happened, because some deny it. I also speak to educate people because some are ignorant about it. For instance, a second-generation Holocaust survivor emailed me her results from interviewing students at Penn State University regarding the Holocaust. Faulty responses from these college students included that the Holocaust took place in the 1800s; blacks were persecuted; and Hitler was a South American ruler! Currently, teaching about the Holocaust is mandatory in only five U.S. states and optional in the others. I speak as much as I can about it, for my greatest hope is that someday there will be peace in the world.

Hard work and persistence, which my father lived and passed onto me, brought our family liberty. Perhaps, if enough people around the world work for peace, the world can be liberated from fighting and flourish in peace.

Today, let's be persistent and work hard to not let the lessons of the past be lost with the passing of time.

VOICE OF TRUTH, VOICE OF PEACE

Bernard Savone
Poland/United States

I grew up in the small town of Chmielnik, Poland. I was the eldest of three other brothers, and my dad worked in the meat business. We were Orthodox Jews, and it was my father who taught us about our religion. I was a teenager when we heard rumors that war was coming. Germany had a new ruler named Adolf Hitler who was mouthing off in speeches that he wanted to get rid of the Jews.

On Friday, September 1, 1939, the German army stormed Poland and brought with them fear, death, and destruction. Because they knew that on Fridays the Jews would be in the synagogue to welcome in the Sabbath with prayer, they set our local synagogue on fire and locked the doors. We had stayed home that night, for my dad had heard rumors something terrible might happen. We watched in horror as the smoke and flames engulfed our friends, and all those inside were killed. The next morning, the Germans imposed curfews on us all, and we were forced to wear the yellow Star of David on the front and back of our clothes to identify us as Jews.

The tyranny continued as the Germans demanded that all the Jews leave their homes with whatever belongings they could carry and led us on a ten kilometer march to Kelce. They put a fence around us and called it a ghetto. The Germans played dirty tricks. When the groceries ran out, they told us that more would be delivered tomorrow, but when tomorrow came, there was no food. This game of false hope continued until people died by the groves.

I learned to be a machinist there and worked in a factory building war equipment. As the camp depleted, the Germans told us they were taking us to Germany for a better life. However, this was just another lie. They crammed us, 150 people tight, standing room only, in a freight train boxcar that reasonably fit fifty people. They told us the trip would take eight hours, but it took two and a half to three days. Screams filled the ride, and many died of starvation and weakness.

Our train then pulled into another camp. The most horrible stench emanated from this camp. It was the most vile thing I have ever smelled. It was like burning oil, rubber, and human waste. Seventy years after first smelling it, I can still smell it. We had arrived at Auschwitz, the death camp, and they were burning human bodies. I remember seeing a soldier dressed in a black uniform with shiny black boots speaking on a loud speaker. It was Dr. Josef Mengele. We called him the "Angel of Death" because he announced who would live and who would die. He commanded the men and women eighteen to thirty years old, "Step to the right," and all others were to step to the left. My father was our family spokesman, and he said, "Listen up. You see the situation. Save yourself anyway you can, and tell the world what one human being can do to another." This became my prayer day and night.

Dr. Mengele pointed for me to go to the right although I wasn't quite eighteen. I was housed in a barrack of fifty with wooden beds three-tiers high. They gave us clothes that look like striped pajamas, and only skimpy, straw mattresses lay upon the bunks. We got up at 5:00 a.m. or sunrise, whichever came first. Each day, we had a small amount of a grainy drink which was supposed to be coffee, but wasn't, a little bit of bread, and vegetable soup.

I was in the Sanitation Unit. As I worked, I saw unbelievable horrors such as men and women being used for target practice. It was my job to bury them after the shootings. One morning, my unit went to the hospital. When I entered, I heard a dreadful noise. Dr. Mengele was doing the most inhumane experiments on prisoners, and they cried out in tortuous pain. As I buried the dead from these experiments, I mumbled to myself, "Nothing can bother me. I must survive to tell the world what one human being can do to another."

As I walked back from the hospital to my barrack, I overheard soldiers saying that my unit was going to be exterminated in a few days so that the secret wouldn't get out about the cruel experiments. I said, "Only a miracle can save me."

I believed in miracles though, and I got my miracle. I saw a rainbow in the sky–the most beautiful rainbow I've ever seen. I was a good student in Hebrew school, and I thought of the story of Noah and the flood, where after the flood ceased, God told Noah that the rainbow was his sign that he would never again destroy people or the earth with a flood. I had lost my faith, but I believed in nature. I walked back to my barrack and repeated my motto, "Stay healthy, obey orders, and try to survive." Then I saw a bulletin board above my barrack door which said there was a need for architects, engineers, and machinists. I told my foreman that I did not belong in the Sanitation Unit for I was a machinist and could help the German war effort. Germany needed skilled workers because all the German males from sixteen to sixty-five were in the armed forces, and only the elderly were in the factories. I was then transported 250 miles away to a factory to make war supplies.

I learned there that not all Germans were murderers. One German woman who worked next to me had tears in her eyes and apologized for what was happening. She said that she did not approve of what the Germans were doing and asked how she could help me. I told her that she'd better not talk like that or she may have a dire fate. She replied that there was nothing the Germans could do to her. She had lost her husband and son. Every morning, she threw a boiled potato in the garbage can outside my barrack where I could retrieve it and eat it. Airplanes later bombed the factory, and I was taken back to my same barrack at Auschwitz. All new people were there. I asked what had happened to the others, and one prisoner pointed to the smokestacks—the gas chambers. Five doctors then came and injected us with typhoid fever as another one of Dr. Mengele's experiments to see how we'd react. After twenty days, only five out of our original forty- eight were still alive.

After recovering from typhoid fever, I told my superior that I was a machinist. I was then sent to an underground factory in a coal mine to make bullets. In January 1945, rumors reached us that Germany was losing the war. The factory commander had received orders to blow up the factory and all the prisoners in it. He had a heart though, so he blew up the factory but not the people. He then put us on a death march back to Auschwitz in the freezing winter months. Auschwitz would not let us in. Corpses were piled building high against the drifts of snow.

On we marched to Kottbus, Germany, which had been heavily bombed, and worked to clean up the city. The Russians were getting close to Germany, so we were taken by train to a desolate area in the mountains between Germany and Austria. The soldiers set up machine guns and started shooting us. When the machine guns got within five feet of me, I heard a loud noise, and the shooting stopped. General Patton's Third

Armored Division of tanks had arrived, and the Germans fled for their lives. When the U.S. GIs saw us, they didn't know how to react to people in our condition. Some cried, others laughed at our skeleton-thin bodies. I was twenty-one years old; five feet, six inches; and weighed a mere sixty-one pounds. One of the captains stood on top of a tank and said, "Shoot those bastards." My thoughts returned to that terrible night in September, watching the synagogue burn with our friends in it. Anger and vengeance rose up in my frail body. I could hardly function, but my brain was working. In Hebrew School, I learned, "Thou shall not kill." If I killed a human being, I would be the same kind of murderer as them, so I did not. The Americans fed us army rations, like sardines and candy bars. I was so hungry that I devoured the candy bars, wrappers and all. I then collapsed and later woke up in a hospital. A doctor told me, "You're one of the lucky ones," because many had died from eating the rich fare.

It was April 1945, and the war was over for us. The U.S. Army declared me a displaced person and told me that I could move to Poland or anywhere in the free world. My first thought now that I was free was to search for my family. Were any still alive? I traveled a thousand miles across Europe and found one of my brothers in Poland. What words could be expressed? We sat on the floor and cried. We quickly left for Munich though, because our lives were threatened by Poles who feared that returning prisoners would reclaim their property. It was in Munich that I was married and had a son. My wife and I then sailed to the United States.

I eventually settled in Denver, Colorado, and fell in love with its beauty. I worked as a butcher and raised my son and daughter there. I loved doing everything with my kids, especially camping. Although I only completed seven grades in school myself, I supported my kids to go to college so they could have every chance at a good life in America. I warned them of the dangers of drugs, and I'm grateful that they're free of such harms.

I also taught them to remember the Holocaust for it's part of our family history, and most of our family perished in it. The most painful and aggravating moment in my life as a father was when my son came home from school and asked why he didn't have a grandfather to bring on Grandparents' Day. It was then I could sit down with him and explain what happened to his family and so many other families in the Holocaust. The same opportunity arose with my daughter when she was young.

When I retired, I began to speak publicly in schools, churches, hospitals, and organizations across the state about the Holocaust and the need for peace. People asked me why I didn't fight back in the camps, and I told them that my speaking was my fighting back. I needed to follow the dictate of my father to tell the world what had happened so that such atrocities can be prevented and peace can fill our future. I taught my kids to work for peace, and my daughter also speaks out about the Holocaust and the need for peace.

I currently reside in California and continue to speak in schools and other organizations. Last year, after I spoke at Los Alamitos High School, a woman came and hugged me. She said, "I am General Patton's granddaughter." History repeated itself, for her grandfather was a force for good in my life, and now his offspring showed her support.

When I speak in schools, I end my talk with, "There is no reason to hate one another; we are created equally. Whether one is black, white, yellow or red, we all love the same, breathe the same, and bleed the same. There are no races, only one race–the human race. As long as we realize that and learn to get along with each other, we will create a better world."

> *J.J. – When I interviewed Bernie, he was full of life at ninety-one. I told him that he had a great memory, and he replied, "You bet ya'!" We spoke at a table in front of a dresser lined with family photos. A family man at heart, his father would be proud of his eldest son who lived his guidance to survive and works to create a better world. When I visited Bernie again to have him review his section of the book, he ended our time with fatherly caring. I'm thin, and he said, "Do something for me. Eat more junk food, and put some meat on your bones." He then gave me a hug and said, "I still love you. Stay well." I returned home and cried feeling so touched by his kindness and blessed by his willingness to tell his story to a stranger in the hope that it can contribute to peace. Bernie's rainbow was a miracle, but his life and wisdom yield the greatest bounty.*

Today, let's be a voice of truth and peace to help create a better world.

> *J.J. – Steven Spielberg filmed videos of Tomas Kovar and Bernard Savone for the USC Shoah Foundation Institute for Visual History and Education which contains audio/visual histories of nearly 52,000 Holocaust survivors and witnesses. The Visual History Archive can be accessed at http://sfi.usc.edu and in locations such as museums and universities throughout the world. Bernard and Tomas participated in this project as another means to educate people about the Holocaust and take a stand for peace.*

EPILOGUE

In 2001, when the idea for this book first came to me and I began interviewing the fathers, I had no idea that it would be a fourteen year journey in the making and would transform my life. Today, upon its publication, I am in awe and humbled by the process. Meeting and talking with fathers all across the globe has changed me and my life forever. I have learned so much about love and life, especially the diverse cultures of all the families involved in this project.

Through compiling *Fathers' Wisdom*, I have experienced a deeper appreciation for adoption and foster parenting, not to mention an eye opening exposure to yoga, meditation, World War II, the Holocaust, and even healthy eating (I'm still a Paleo gal!). I feel I have traveled through new worlds and visited foreign countries all through the experiences of these wonderful fathers. I have navigated these years through California sites and homes, international calling plans, politics, religion, marriage, and relationships. My vehicle being cell phones, texting, computers, websites, social media, businesses, museums, science, the planets, the universe, interviewing, networking and the lives of these amazing fathers!

I have put on many hats in this fourteen year process–project management, researching, cold calling, writing, marketing, and publishing. My home is filled with stacks of interviews that have overflowed my desk, coffee table, and storage cupboard. The list could go on and on. But it is the fathers and the many people who have contributed to this book who have enriched my life by their stories and their willingness to help with a project honoring the priceless treasure of family and the wisdom of fathers that have made such an everlasting imprint upon me.

When people ask me what I've learned from doing this book, I reply, "All fathers are the same, and all fathers are different." They all love their children but in their own special way.

Today, I am in awe of fathers. I smile every time I think of their love, commitment and dedication to nurture, protect, educate, and provide for their children. The men in this book represent humanity at its best—men who love their children and honor their responsibilities with their families, profession, community and world-at-large. I love all these fathers, and they became a special group for me—a family of fathers united by the call and duty of being a father.

Our world is filled with stories of parents not living up to their responsibilities, but our world is also filled with parents who do. These fathers do, and I have offered their stories to you, to inspire you to pursue your dreams and to live each day a little more wise, a little more healthy and full of joy. The fathers' love overflows in their stories, and now I hope it flows into your hearts, minds, and lives.

I wish you all blessings of *Fathers' Wisdom.*

—

Jennifer Jordan
Adoring daughter and celebrator of fathers!

At **SQUARE TREE PUBLISHING,** we believe that your message matters. That is why our dedicated team of professionals is committed to bringing your literary texts and targeted curriculum to a global marketplace. We strive to make that message of the highest quality, while still maintaining your voice. We believe in you, therefore, we provide a platform through website design, blogs, and social media campaigns to showcase your unique message. Our innovative team offers a full range of services from editing to graphic design inspired with an eye for excellence, so that your message is clearly and distinctly heard.

Whether you are a new writer needing guidance with each step of the process, or a seasoned writer, we will propel you to the next level of your development. At **SQUARE TREE PUBLISHING,** it's all about you!

Take advantage of a free consultation.
Your opportunity is "Write Outside the Box!"
WWW.SQUARETREEPUBLISHING.COM

Made in the USA
Charleston, SC
20 June 2015